MILL AND
LIBERALISM

2

MILL AND LIBERALISM

BY

MAURICE COWLING

Fellow of Peterhouse, Cambridge, and formerly
Fellow of Jesus College, Cambridge

SECOND EDITION

The right of the
University of Cambridge
to print and sell
all manner of books
was granted by
Henry VIII in 1534.
The University has printed
and published continuously
since 1584.

CAMBRIDGE UNIVERSITY PRESS

Cambridge
New York   Port Chester
Melbourne   Sydney

Published by the Press Syndicate of the University of Cambridge
The Pitt Building, Trumpington Street, Cambridge CB2 1RP
40 West 20th Street, New York, NY 10011, USA
10 Stamford Road, Oakleigh, Melbourne 3166, Australia

First published 1963

This edition first published 1990

Printed in Great Britain at the Bath Press, Avon

British Library cataloguing in publication data

Cowling, Maurice, 1926–
Mill and liberalism. – 2nd ed.
1. English philosophy. Mill, John Stuart, 1806–1873
1. Title
192

Library of Congress cataloguing in publication data

Cowling, Maurice,
Mill and liberalism/by Maurice Cowling. – 2nd ed.
p.   cm.
ISBN 0 521 38219 X – ISBN 0 521 38872 4 (pbk)
1. Mill, John Stuart, 1806–1873 – Contributions in political
science. 2. Liberty 3. Liberalism. I. Title.
JC223.M66C69   1989
323.44 – dc20   89–35677   CIP

ISBN 0 521 38219 X hard covers
ISBN 0 521 38872 4 paperback

CONTENTS

I. EXPOSITION

II. CRITICISM

It is an inevitable mark of what the late Sir Edwyn Hoskyns used to call the 'tyranny of liberalism' that the liberal is not only convinced that he is right; he is also convinced that other people secretly agree with him—how could they do otherwise?—and are only restrained from saying so by unworthy motives arising from wordly prudence, material interest, and so forth.

c. h. smyth, 'The Importance of Church Attendance' in
The Recall to Religion, London 1937, p. 120.

About the Essays dear, would not religion, the Utility of Religion, be one of the subjects you would have most to say on ... to account for the existence nearly universal of some religion (superstition) by the instincts of fear, hope and mystery, etc., and throwing over all doctrines and theories, called religion as devices for power ... to show how religion and poetry fill the same want, the craving after higher objects, the consolation of suffering, the hope of heaven for the selfish, love of God for the tender and grateful—how all this must be superseded by morality deriving its power from sympathies and benevolence and its reward from the approbation of those we respect.

There, what a long-winded sentence ...

Harriet Taylor to Mill, 14–15 February 1854.
f. a. hayek, *John Stuart Mill and Harriet Taylor*, London 1951, pp. 195–6
(with emendation).

Philip thought this over for a moment, then he said:
'I don't see why the things we believe absolutely now shouldn't be just as wrong as what they believed in the past.'
'Neither do I.'
'Then how can you believe anything at all?'
'I don't know.'

w. somerset maugham, *Of Human Bondage*,
London 1915, p. 121.

PREFACE TO THE FIRST EDITION

The author is grateful to Mrs I. M. Martin of Cambridge for typing this book and to the Syndics of the University Press for publishing it. He owes a large debt to Mr J. A. Tuck for very kindly reading the proofs, to Professor J. M. Robson of Toronto for verifying an emendation (quoted on p. ix), and to Mr Kedourie, Professor Oakeshott, Mr I. R. Willison and Professor Karl Britton for commenting on the manuscript. More general obligations have been recorded in another work.

MAURICE COWLING

JESUS COLLEGE
CAMBRIDGE
May 1963

PREFACE TO THE
SECOND EDITION

(i)

Mill and Liberalism, written very rapidly a year earlier, was published in November 1963. At that time many things were in the future the occurrence of which may obscure the fact that, so far from being merely about Mill, it was about a phase in the development of the English public mind – that consensual phase in which the socialism, liberal collectivism and international anti-totalitarianism which had been established with the 1940 coalition had provided the over-arching norm of English public thought for nearly twenty-five years.[1]

By November 1963, Gaitskell had died and Macmillan had resigned, but the Wilson primeministership had not begun and had not yet created the moral depression it was to create on the Liberal Left. Ulster had not become a desert, nor Mr Heath leader of the Conservative Party. Powellism was only a gleam in the eye and Thatcherism was not even that. There had been no exodus from the Labour Party, Owenism and Thatcherism had not become havens for exiles, and the Conservative Party had neither tamed the trade unions nor established the ascendancy it was to establish in the 1980s. The ghosts of Tawney, Beveridge and Keynes were still at large, as were Koestler,

[1] The author is grateful for the help he has received in writing this preface from Lord Bauer, Mr Guy Black, Dr Alistair Cooke, Dr Patrick Cosgrave, Mr Charles Covell, Lord Harris of High Cross, Dr Ian Harris, Mr Robin Harris, Mr Frank Johnson, Dr Sheila Lawlor, Mrs Shirley Letwin, Mr John O'Sullivan, Canon James Owen, Dr Jonathan Parry, the Rt Hon. J. Enoch Powell, Professor Roger Scruton, Mr Ronald Spark, Professor and Mrs John Vincent, Dr David Watkin, Dr J. A. Weir and Mr John Wood. As so often before, he is indebted to Mrs H. M. Dunn for typing.

Snow, Ayer, Hampshire, Jenkins, Crosland, Shonfield, Kahn, Balogh, Kaldor, Joan Robinson, J. K. Galbraith and David Astor. Popper had not been converted, Annan and Beloff had not been ennobled, and Berlin was running ostentatiously against the current he was as conspicuously running with. There were few signs of the Student Revolution and the reign of priggishness, puritanism and permissiveness which were to accompany it. Though Raymond Williams was about to become a guru, it was by no means obvious that Hobsbawm, Anderson, Eagleton and Thompson would become gurus too. The opinions which had become average as the student revolution of the 1930s had become the middle-aged Keynesianism of the 1950s, still seemed to be delivering the goods and seemed likely to go on doing so, morally, politically, and intellectually, into the far distant future. No-one yet understood that anti-totalitarianism, the memory of the war and 'the end of ideology' were propping them up, or that resuscitation after the 'death' of political theory might end by subverting them.

That in effect is what has happened. Professor Bernard Williams has made gestures of defence and has been assisted in his gesturings by Professor Dunn's negativity, by Professor Skinner's civic trifles, and by the broader liberalism of Mr Runciman and Professor Rawls. But the orthodoxy has been eroded, by political and economic events and by intellectual transactions not only on the Right, among converted Socialists and on the Marxist Left, but also, via Hayek and Nozick, from within Liberalism itself. It is undoubtedly the case that collectivism and the higher Liberalism smelt a very great deal fresher twenty-five years ago than they do now.

Collectivism is one thing, the higher Liberalism is another. While *implying* an attitude towards the former, *Mill and Liberalism* was primarily about the latter.

For *Mill and Liberalism* the real world was not a liberal world, as the Marxists of the late 1960s were also to point out. It treated Liberalism as an élitist delusion and implied that it was Christianity which should underpin national solidarity. The Christianity it envisaged was Anglican and lacked the liberal appendages with which almost all types of Christianity have come to be lumbered since Pope John XXIII. Even so, the idea of a Christian society was as eccentric as the ideas it was attacking since, by 1963, perhaps even by 1903, a populist Anglican Christianity had become a chimaera.

About religion, *Mill and Liberalism* was nostalgic. Intellectually it was aggressive. It continued the attack which had been mounted crudely, in Oakeshottian language, and with more heat than light, against the 'statesmen in disguise' who had been pilloried in *The Nature and Limits of Political Science* six months earlier, and it argued that Mill had not only been advocating a post-Christian religion, which he had pretended duplicitously not to be advocating, but had also suffused his advocacy with the same sort of liberal intolerance with which the higher Liberals and liberal collectivists in all political parties and all parts of the intellectual spectrum in the 1950s, had been suffusing theirs. Liberal intolerance and self-contradiction were the targets, or rather the inability of the liberal mind to understand that relativism and the sociology of knowledge could be turned against it, that the last king did not *have* to be strangled with the entrails of the last priest, and that, since arbitrariness was a characteristic of *all* assumptions, liberal assumptions (in the absence of the numinousness which they had sometimes had in the past but no longer had now) had none of the authority which was claimed for them.

Mill and Liberalism was no more designed to make readers aprove of Mill than *The Nature and Limits of Political Science* had been designed to make them approve of Myrdal, Lady

xi

Wootton or Sir Ivor Jennings. Though the authorial intention was devious, the consequence was empathetic. *Mill and Liberalism* described the religious nature of Mill's coherence, the proselytising function of his libertarianism, and the *odium theologicum* which had impregnated his emasculation of Christianity, and it concluded that, though contentious and at lower levels incoherent, the most important feature of Mill's thought at an important level was its coherence, not just as a matter of intention but through the more important sap which seeps from the pores of all thinkers, whether they intend it to or not.

Mill and Liberalism was written without any expectation either that truth would be rewarded or that consequences would ensue. There was no desire to produce consequences, there was an innocent desire not to, and there was a crooked claim that academic understanding would be promoted by not doing so. Though 'academic' needed to be differentiated from 'liberal', there was not much to be said, except tactically, in favour of the disconnection between explanatory, or academic, writing on the one hand and writing designed to persuade or have practical consequences on the other, and there was a great deal to be said for the view, of which the crookedness only marginally inhibited understanding, that practice and theory, however devious their interconnections, are inseparably interconnected, even in universities.

When *Mill and Liberalism* was reviewed, several reviewers identified themselves as archetypes of its targets, one of them describing it, obligingly, as 'dangerous and unpleasant', which was what it was intended to be.[2] Since then the already massive literature about Mill has proliferated, some of it in ways which are consonant with *Mill and*

[2] For 'dangerous and unpleasant' see Dr Roland Hall in *Philosophical Quarterly*, January 1965. Lord Annan, Professor Cranston, Professor Ryan, Professor Wollheim and the young Dr Lukes also identified *themselves* in *The Observer, The Listener, New Statesman and Nation* and *New Society*.

Liberalism, more of it in ways which are not. One feature of most of it has been that it deals with bits and pieces of Mill, or problems in Mill, and does not achieve a synthetic interpretation of Mill. That *Mill and Liberalism* does achieve a synthetic interpretation by contextualising Mill, understanding him as a cultural elitist, and drawing out the anti-Christian implications of the sociological philosophy he wished to inject into aristocratic mindlessness, commercial philistinism and the as yet unrealised intellectuality of the poor is its main merit and the chief reason for thinking it as central an introduction to Mill's thought as when it was written twenty-five years ago.

If *Mill and Liberalism* were being written now, it would be more circuitous about Mill's view of the clerisy and more comprehensive about his philosophy, would give closer attention to Bentham, James Mill and Carlyle, to the history and varieties of Liberalism, and to Mill's interest in India, France, economics and literature, and, while continuing to present Mill's libertarianism as an instrument of intellectual unanimity in the long run, would be slower to impute instrumentality in the short run. In the main, however, it would reaffirm its account of Mill's hostility to Christianity and ignorance of Christianity's vitality, would enlarge on the intimacy of the connection he assumed between the libertarian principle, the 'Art of Life' and the obsolescence of Christianity, and would justify the enlargement not only as a matter of psychological plausibility but also by reference to the intimacies which *Religion and Public Doctrine in Modern England* was to impute to many other Victorian and twentieth-century thinkers from 1980 onwards. Above all, it would state, more emphatically but more subtly than in 1963, that the object in writing was to show how rancid secular intelligentsias are capable of being, and how rancid they have been, in taking up the burden of reconstructing the thought-world which 1517, the 1680s, 1789 or 1917 are supposed to have destroyed.

The Nature and Limits of Political Science and *Mill and Liberalism* were brash essays in debt repayment, which were to be continued in *Religion and Public Doctrine*, vol. 1, later.[3] They also transposed onto an academic plane the arguments of a pamphlet the author had written six years earlier in criticism of the outrage that had been provoked in liberal minds in all political parties and all areas of British life by Eden's attempt to use military force to reoccupy the Suez Canal and bring down the Nasser government in October 1956.[4]

The pamphlet reflected the intensity of anger which was felt by both the critics and the supporters of Eden during the Suez crisis. The pamphlet was not a defence of Eden; far less was it a defence of his cooperation with Israel. It was anti-Israeli, mindful of the dubiousness of Israeli claims and the success of Israeli propaganda, and mistrustful of Eden's opportunism. Its main arguments were of two conflicting kinds – on the one hand that Britain was a third-class power which could probably not afford to exercise paramountcy in the Middle East and would be unable to do so in the future if it failed to do so on this occasion; on the other hand, that it was intellectually disreputable to pretend, as Eden's critics had pretended, that the United Nations transcended conventional diplomacy and the interests of states, or supplied such superior guarantees of World-Order that Britain should never use military force against states which attacked her interests.

These were judgments on the way. The fundamental judgment was that an intelligentsia which could work up

[3] In chapters 3–5 and 10–11 particularly.

[4] The pamphlet, invited by the then director of the Conservative Political Centre, was written in a partisan tone, and was obviously unpublishable at a time in early 1957 when the prevailing desire of the Conservative Party was to get as far away from Suez as possible.

the moral indignation that the English intelligentsia had worked up in late 1956 was so narrow and naive as to be culturally offensive.

It is difficult after more than thirty years to recreate the process through which a pamphlet about Suez became a book about Mill. But there certainly was a connection, and it was a connection of cultural distaste. It carried over into the belief, which was to be developed in *The Impact of Hitler* in 1975, that, from Britain's point of view the 1939 war had been a liberal war which had been entered into in a condition of moral indignation without the resources to fight it, that it had been providential good fortune which had placed the burden of fighting on the Russians and the Americans, and that the unjustifiable complacency which victory had inserted into the British mind demanded special resources of illusionlessness and hardmindedness, and an intellectual grasp of the insecurity of British prosperity and power, if British politics were to be conducted sensibly in the future.

In the decade after *Mill and Liberalism* the author wrote three works in which an actual (or historical) as opposed to an exhortatory (or Skinnerian) contextualisation was applied to three English situations – the emergence of Disraeli and Gladstone as party leaders in the 1860s, the emergence of Labour as a governing party in the 1920s, and the emergence of Churchill and Labour in a governing coalition in 1940. There were real contributions to political understanding. It is as true now as it was twenty years ago that public speech in a democracy is functional, that democratic speech conceals both its hand and its mind, and that democratic politicians have both conventions and an 'autonomy' which require for their appreciation a comprehension as critical as the comprehension required for the appreciation of poetry.

For proposing procedures of sceptical diagnosis, the

author became typecast as part of a 'Peterhouse school of history' which was supposed to be treating parliamentary politics as a Namieriate venality, though it owed nothing directly to Namier, treated parliament as an instrument of class warfare, and, so far as it treated parliamentary politics as a spectacle of ambition and manoeuvre, was borrowing from Mr Henry Fairlie (the political columnist of *The Spectator* in the 1950s) and from the central chapters of *The Unknown Prime Minister* which Lord Blake had published in confirmation of his own and Beaverbrook's methodological instincts in 1955.[5] An essay in a Powellite volume of 1970,[6] a year as literary editor of Mr Gale's *Spectator*, and a volume of *Conservative Essays*[7] which fired ill-sighted shots across the bows of the *economic* 'New Right',[8] had meanwhile typecast the author as part of a

[5] Others who have been similarly typecast include Professor John Vincent of the University of Bristol, Dr A. B. Cooke (the present director of the Conservative Political Centre), late of Queen's University, Belfast, Dr Andrew Jones (the distinguished bookseller) late of the University of Reading, Dr Jonathan Clark of All Souls College, Oxford, Dr Jonathan Parry of King's College, London, Dr Philip Williamson of the University of Durham, Dr Richard Brent, late of St John's College, Cambridge, and Dr Michael Bentley of the University of Sheffield, all of whom apart from Dr Bentley were either undergraduates or Fellows of Peterhouse. They have written, among other works, *The Formation of the Liberal Party* and *Disraeli* (Vincent), *The Governing Passion* (Vincent and Cooke), *The Politics of Reform* (Jones), *Politics Without Democracy*, *The Liberal Mind 1914–29* and *The Climax of Liberal Policy* (Bentley), *The Dynamics of Change, English Society 1660–1832* and *Revolution and Rebellion* (Clark), *Democracy and Religion* (Parry), *Liberal Anglican Politics* (Brent) and *National Crisis and National Government 1927–1932* (forthcoming, or so it seems, from Williamson). If these are read together and in conjunction with the present author's *Disraeli, Gladstone and Revolution*, *The Impact of Labour*, *The Impact of Hitler* and *Religion and Public Doctrine in Modern England*, it will be obvious that the typecast, if it ever bore any relation to reality, no longer does so.
[6] 'The Present Situation' in *Powell and the 1970 Election*, edited by Mr John Wood of the Institute of Economic Affairs, which also included contributions by Mr George Gale and Mrs Diana Spearman.
[7] With contributions from Mrs Shirley Letwin, Mr T. E. Utley, Dr Edward Norman, Professor Kenneth Minogue, Mr Gale, Mr Peregrine Worsthorne, Dr Bentley, Dr Jones, Professor Roger Scruton, Dr John Casey, Mr John Biffen, M.P., Professor Richard Griffiths and the late Lord Peyton, the first twelve of whom appear elsewhere in this introduction.
[8] As was suggested by both Mr Samuel Brittan (*Encounter*, January 1980, p. 42) and Mr Arthur Seldon of the Institute of Economic Affairs who, in the Institute's coming-of-age volume, *Confrontation*, in 1978 (p. 22) identified *Conservative Essays* not only with Sir Ian Gilmour's Conservatism, which the editor of *Conservative Essays* particularly disliked, but also with Mr William Waldegrave's *Binding of Leviathan* which, when suggested by

political 'New Right' about which, though there have been many accounts,[9] there has been much misunderstanding.

(ii)

During the past twenty-five years there have been many shifts of mentality which, if given more central political expression, might have constituted the basis for a 'New Right'. Professor Greenleaf's Oakeshottian anti-collectivism and the anti-collectivism of *The Economic History Review* under Dr Max Hartwell and Professor C. H. Wilson are examples. So are the Larkinian pessimism which transported Mr Kingsley Amis from the Fabian Society to the Black Papers, the adaptations of

Professor Scruton for inclusion in an abridged form in *Conservative Essays*, had seemed to be insufficiently in sympathy with the other contributions to be included. *The Binding of Leviathian* offered an attractive but uncynical and uncomplicated intellectualisation of an organic rural Conservatism which did not, as it seemed, provide an adequate framework for the understanding of modern, urban, Jacobin politics.

[9] For misunderstandings see especially D. Edgar, 'Bitter harvest' in ed. James Curran, *The Future of the Left*, and *The Second Time as Farce*. Desmond King, *The New Right*, realises that there are differences between Conservative politicians and the academic Right but, like Andrew Gamble, *The Free Economy and the Strong State*, and Robert Leach (in M. Burch and M. Moran, *British Politics, A Reader*) does not understand that the main difference is a difference in political importance. There are sensible observations in Noel O'Sullivan's essay (in ed. J. Hayward and P. Norton, *The Political Science of British Politics*). *The Redefinition of Conservatism* by Charles Covell, who knows some of the authors it discusses, has the merit, among others, of not imagining that they have been important politically. S. Hall and M. Jacques, *The Politics of Thatcherism*, P. Dunleavy and B. O'Leary *Theories of the State*, and Nicholas Bosanquet, *After the New Right*, very properly ignore the non-economic New Right. D. Kavanagh, *Thatcherism in British Politics*, exaggerates the authoritarianism of *Conservatism Essays* and misses Professor Scruton's idiosyncrasy. So really does R. Levitas, *The Ideology of the New Right*. None of these, nor Professor R. Plant (in Drucker, Dunleavy, Gamble and Peele, *Developments in British Politics, A Reader*), has any sense of the significance of the cultural, religious and 'high-political' assumptions which were inseparable from *Conservative Essays*. There is a tendency in much left-wing analysis to overestimate the novelty of the New Right, even of the economic New Right, and to ignore the extent to which its 'new ideas' can be found in the thought, rhetoric and practice of the Conservative Party throughout the twentieth century. John Vincent, 'The Thatcher Governments', in ed. P. Hennessey and Anthony Seldon, *Ruling Performances*, supplies a corrective. In the early 1980s there were informed newspaper articles by Mr Godfrey Hodgson in *The Sunday Times Magazine* and by Mr Martin Walker in *The Guardian*.

Leavis made by Mr Ian Robinson and *The Human World*, and the aesthetic leap which has enabled Mr Peter Fuller to move from the Marxism of his first ten books to become the Scrutonian founder of *Modern Painters* and art critic of *The Sunday Telegraph*. Among the Roman Catholic and Anglican laity there has been resistance to the liberalism and collectivism of the higher clergy and, among Anglican ordinands and the Anglican well-to-do, an Evangelical, Sabbatarian and biblical-Calvinist revival which has been both politically Conservative and more theocratic than Mrs Mary Whitehouse, from an older generation of Evangelicals, had ever wished to be. *Private Eye* and Mr Alan Watkins of *The Observer*, though differing from one other and not in either case being Conservative, have had conservative resonances, while the sociological relativism which has underpinned the successive versions of the New Left could equally well have underpinned a Tory Marxism dedicated to the cynical truth, which English Marxists are too liberal to appreciate, that the inequalities, sufferings and alienations consequent upon ideological hegemony are vital concomitants of the freedom, discipline and social solidarity of modern societies.

There have been by-blows. Essentially, the New Right in these years has had five faces, all of which have manifested passion and conviction, even where there has also been mistrust of passion and conviction, and all of which have set themselves to wrench the public mind out of the groove it had been running in since 1940. These are, the movement of economic opinion against Keynesianism, corporatism and collectivism and in favour of capitalism, monetarism and the free market; the parliamentary, party and public movements known as Powellism and Thatcherism; the educational movement which derives from the Black Papers; the movement of academic opinion which is known severally as the Peterhouse Right, the

London School of Economics Right and Professor Scruton's Right; and a movement among Conservative journalists associated primarily with the *Daily* and *Sunday Telegraph*s.

The economic movement was the expression of judgments made by historians like Ashton and Hartwell that the Industrial Revolution, so far from destroying the living standards of the poor, had rescued the English poor from the poverty which the poor had suffered in Ireland and India. It was also the expression of judgments made by economists like Jewkes, Schwartz, Bauer, Hayek, von Mises, Robbins and Sir Dennis Robertson, that Keynes did not deserve to displace Adam Smith, that the collectivist orthodoxy was mistaken, and that the Treasury, all the political parties, and most economics faculties in British universities, were in supine subservience to it. These were the judgments which had been given wide circulation by Hayek's book *The Road to Serfdom* in 1944 and received a propaganda-edge when Mr Anthony Fisher incorporated and Lord Harris set up the Institute of Economic Affairs between 1955 and 1957.

The I.E.A. was a non-party body and included among its members economists with varied political involvements, including Liberals like Sir Oscar Hobson and ex-socialists like Hutton, Nash and Colin Clark. Mr Arthur Seldon belonged to the Liberal party and Lord Harris to the Conservative party; Mr John Wood, who eventually became the third full-time member, did not belong to any party.[10] Wood was at Oundle, Harris and Seldon at

[10] Harris and Seldon are authors, together and separately, of innumerable books and pamphlets, including *Politics Without Prejudice, Advertising in A Free Society, Hire Purchase In A Free Society, Pensions For Prosperity, Advertising And The Public, After the N.H.S., Choice in Welfare, The Great Pensions Swindle, Over-Ruled in Welfare, Whither the Welfare State?*, (ed.) *The New Right Enlightenment, Not From Benevolence, Challenge Of A Radical Reactionary, Beyond The Welfare State*, etc. etc. Wood is the author of *How Much Unemployment?, How Little Unemployment,* (with G. Polanyi) *How Much Inequality?*, (with R. Miller) *Exchange Control For Ever?* and (with R. Miller) *What Price Unemployment?* etc. he has also edited a number of volumes of Mr Powell's speeches.

London grammar schools. All three had read Economics, Seldon at the London School of Economics in the 1930s when Hayek was a Professor, Wood in Cambridge in the late 1940s under S. R. Dennison, for whom he had worked in the Cabinet Office after reading Politics, Philosophy and Economics at Oxford, Harris in Cambridge at the same time under Hagenbuch and Dennison.

After Cambridge Harris was a lecturer in Political Economy at St Andrews, a Conservative parliamentary candidate in Scotland, and a biographer of Lord Butler at a time when Lord Butler could easily be represented – in the way in which Messrs Maudling, Macleod and Powell were to represent him by contrast with Lord Home seven years later – as a thinking Conservative and the natural Conservative leader. It would have been appropriate if Lord Harris had been as much turned off when the author of *The Middle Way* became Prime Minister in January 1957 as he was to be turned on when Lord Thorneycroft, Lord Rhyl (Mr Nigel Birch) and Mr Enoch Powell – the Macmillan Treasury team – resigned from the Macmillan government a year later.

The I.E.A.'s aim was to have an impact on Westminster and Whitehall. But in its early years it did not see its way. It published books and pamphlets which subjected the consensus to critical examination, first by economists,[11] later by non-economists as well.[12] It developed connections with Lord Grimond, Lord Wyatt and Mr Desmond Donnelly (these last two when they were Labour M.P.s), persuaded Mr Powell, Lord Thorneyc-

[11] E.g. Messrs Hutt, Morgan, Shenfield, Yamey, Prest, Paish, Bareau, Stigler, Johnson, Walters, Peacock, Friedman, Hayek and J. M. Buchanan (before he became famous), to whom Messrs Preston, Minford, Brittan, Brian Griffiths and Rees-Mogg were to be added later, along, more marginally, with Messrs Jay and Oppenheimer. (The weight and intelligence of I.E.A. pamphlets in the middle and later 1970s is very striking.
[12] Including over the years Professor Julius Gould, Dr Hartwell, Mr Ronald Butt, Mr Colin Welch, Mr Andrew Alexander and Professor Norman Gash – the distinguished historian who, when he joined it, was one of the few dons to belong to the Carlton Club.

roft, Lord Shawcross and Sir Alan Herbert to write for it, and was approached spontaneously both by Sir Geoffrey Howe, when chairman of the Bow Group, and by Lord Joseph after the general election of 1964. In general, on the other hand, its managers despaired of politicians' indifference to economic argument, mistrusted the Conservative party's subservience to farmers' interests and the Labour Party's subservience to Trade Union interests, and doubted for a very long time whether two London grammar-school boys and one public-school boy would be able to convert the massed ranks of an Establishment consensus.

In the 1960s the I.E.A. was radical in the way in which *Mill and Liberalism* was radical: it wanted to blow up the consensus, though the consensus it wanted to blow up was the collectivist consensus about economic policy rather than the liberal-internationalist consensus about Suez. Having set out (in Harris's case, at least) with Robbins as its mentor and Keynes, Beveridge and Galbraith as its targets, it found in Hayek's book *The Constitution of Liberty*, which left the present author cold when it was published in 1960, a constructive statement which transcended the negative statement that Hayek had made in *The Road to Serfdom* sixteen years earlier.[13]

At first the I.E.A. emphasised not so much liberty and economic growth as economic truth – or rather the macro-economic distortions on which Keynesianism was founded. A micro-economic analysis then became the guarantor of entrepreneurial growth, consumer liberty and reduced taxation, and was accompanied by assaults – on the special interests which were being encouraged to carry begging bowls around government departments, on the statistics with which government departments were

[13] For Hayek and the Institute of Economic Affairs see esp. (ed.) A. Seldon, *Agenda for Liberty*, and (ed.) J. Burton, *Hayek's Serfdom Revisited*.

anaesthetising the public, and on the claim that a mixed economy was better able than a capitalist economy to maintain economic prosperity.

During the Macmillan years the I.E.A. was marginal. Though conscious of a change in economic assumptions in the Conservative Party after the general election of 1964, it felt little confidence in Mr Heath's economic conversion, was depressed by his policies after 1972, and did not begin to feel central until Lord Joseph's second conversion in 1974 and the International Monetary Fund's judgment on the economic events of the 1970s, seemed to prove that what it had been saying was true.

Since the mid-1970s the I.E.A. has been an impressive publishing undertaking, has felt itself a great deal closer than in the 1950s to professional economic opinion (in the Virginian version especially), and has seen many aspects of its thought, and some of its policies, made part of Conservative and governmental thought and policy. Though it has failed, if it tried, to convert the Labour Party, the identity between its language and intentions and the language and intentions of Mrs Thatcher's government has become very close.

Parallel to the I.E.A., but more amateur and a decade later in origin, have been the Black Papers. These were published first during the Student Revolution of 1968 by Dr A. E. Dyson and Professor C. B. Cox who, with the further assistance of Sir Rhodes Boyson in the 1970s, attracted a collection of trans-party contributors including Warden Sparrow, Professor Eysenck, Miss Iris Murdoch, Mr Amis, Mr Gross, Dr Conquest, Dr Lakatos, the Reverend Dr Edward Norman, Dr Bryan Wilson and Lord Beloff.[14]

Dyson and Cox belonged to the English Faculty at

[14] Lord Beloff, having cooperated with Lord Harris, Sir Sydney Caine, Dr D. R. Denman and Professor H. S. Ferns (the ex-Marxist historian of Latin America) and others in setting up the privately funded University of Buckingham, became its first

Manchester University and had been editing *The Critical Quarterly* for a decade when the Student Revolution began. They believed that the ultimate effect of the revolution would be to reduce state funding and academic independence, and they were led on by the success of a Black Paper about University Education into Black Papers about School Education which claimed that numeracy and literacy were being neglected and that comprehensivisation, as it was actually being carried out, would reduce standards and deprive able working-class children of access to the universities.

Dyson and Cox were Labour voters who had been brought up on Leavis in Cambridge but had broken the mould and been much influenced by Barzun and Hannah Arendt. Sir Rhodes Boyson, before he became an M.P. and a Conservative Minister, had written economic history,[15] had been headmaster of a comprehensive school in London, and had learned to speak the language of Tory populism. Between them these three identified a crisis and the need to replace the delinquency and liberation which they associated with progressive education by discipline, northern earnestness and parental and institutional authority. In the late 1960s and early 1970s they attracted attention from school teachers and the media and, while having virtually no organisation and making no impact on policy,[16] had a considerable impact on public debate, especially during Mr Callaghan's prime ministership.

Principal nearly a decade after the Home government's acceptance of the Robbins Report and the consequent expansion in the number of state-funded universities had had the effect (paradoxically in view of Lord Robbins's involvement) of making it difficult to suppose that there was any need for new private universities, except as a demonstration of the possibility of a free market in higher education in the future.

[15] I.e. *The North East Lancashire Poor Law 1838–1871* and *The Ashworth Cotton Enterprise.* Sir Rhodes's subsequent works include (ed.) *Down With the Poor, Centre Forward,* (ed.) *Goodbye to Nationalisation,* (ed.) *Right Turn, Oversubscribed,* (ed.) *1985* and (ed.) *Education: The Threatened Standards.*

[16] Which, except financially, and apart from the attack on the grammar schools, continued on the lines laid down by Lord Butler for schools in 1944 and Lord Robbins for universities in 1964.

The Black Paper movement, though not important in itself, was a symptom of distaste for 'progressive' education.[17] It showed that there was a reactionary public waiting to be tapped, as it had been waiting since the Smethwick by-election of 1965, that the instinct which had led Mr Powell to try to tap it was a sure one, and that the contradictions which were to be exemplified later by Mr Honeyford from a tolerable, and Mr Rushdie from an odious, standpoint, were implicit in the Indian, Pakistani and West Indian immigrations, the size of which Mr Powell had denounced the Home Office for wilfully under-estimating from 1968 onwards.

Powellism was Mr Powell's attempt to establish himself as Conservative leader, to revivify Conservative policy, and to put the Conservative Party in tune with popular opinion after the Conservative defeat at the general election of 1966. This was attractive to some economists but objectionable to others because it associated the new economic norms which Mr Heath was also adopting with Mr Powell's illiberal Nietzscheanism. Though unsuccessful in promoting Mr Powell, it induced public intolerance of the consensus he was attacking and the first widespread feeling that liberal rhetoric, and particularly Mr Heath's liberal rhetoric, was intolerable.

Mr Powell's appeal, though idiosyncratic, was broad-based. It was attractive intellectually by reason of the impression Mr Powell left of having democratic, perhaps even nihilistic, instincts, of being clever enough and nasty enough to stand out against consensual wisdom, and, like Mrs Thatcher later, of not being part of a bureaucratic establishment.

In becoming a public idol, Mr Powell came to be in permanent rebellion against Mr Heath. He joined other

[17] For example, on the part of Dr John Marks, Baroness Cox and the National Council for Educational Standards with which Sir Rhodes Boyson has also been associated.

Conservative MPs in voting with the Labour Party about issues like the Prices and Incomes Policy, developed an unexpected solidarity with the Ulster Unionist Party after the suppression of the Stormont parliament in 1972, and 10-operated silently, via Mr Andrew Alexander (then of the *Yorkshire Post*) with Mr Wilson and the Labour Party about the European Economic Community at the first general election of 1974. Despite having a small parliamentary following independently of issues, he did not develop a party within the Party and, instead of fighting the 1974 election at the head of a Conservative group committed to vote together on European issues afterwards, resigned from the Conservative Party and urged electors to vote Labour. In this phase of activity, apart from Mr Biffen and others in the House of Commons, Mr Powell had an embryonic intelligentsia outside, including Messrs Wood and Alexander along, in their congruent but personally more distant ways, with Messrs Gale, Lejeune, Butt, Cosgrave, Harrington, Welch, Utley and some of the other journalists who later became supporters of Mrs Thatcher.

As a concept 'Thatcherism' was almost certainly invented by critics on the Left and implies a continuity of intention which historical investigation may be inclined to question. It is certain, however, that the Centre for Policy Studies was invented by Lord Joseph (and Mrs Thatcher) as a makeweight to the Conservative Research Department after Mr Heath's first general election defeat in 1974, that its public purpose was to proclaim Capitalism's superiority to Socialism, and that the original intention was to start with a 'great debate' in the Albert Hall between Lord Joseph and Mr Michael Foot. An Eysenckian, or Eugenic, speech drafted for him by Sir Alfred Sherman having then compelled Lord Joseph to retire, Mrs Thatcher led the attack on Mr Heath, benefiting in the contest for the Conservative leadership not only from the fact that she was not Mr Heath (who was by now widely disliked in the Conservative Party) but also from her willingness to suggest regret for the traumas and tergiversations through which Conservatives had been made, humourlessly, to pass in the later years of Mr Heath's government, of which, of course, she had been a member.

In opposition between 1975 and 1979 the Centre for Policy Studies[18] took over some of the Institute of Economic Affairs's authors and much of what they had established, and supplemented the economic justification they had been offering of the new economic norms with an attempt to provide a 'moral' justification as well. The outcome was the establishment of a low-keyed powerhouse, in which Mrs Thatcher (and Lord Joseph) rehearsed the arguments they were to act on in office, and a publishing imprint was supplied for pamphlets by Mr Congdon, Mr Russell Lewis, Mr Samuel Brittan, Mr Amis, Lord Bauer, Lord Thomas, Lord Bruce-Gardyne and Lord Joseph, as well as for collections of speeches by Mr Biffen and Mrs Thatcher.

Until enough of the archives are open, including the private archives of politicians, it will be difficult to know how Mrs Thatcher succeeded after 1979 in effecting changes which Mr Heath had promised in 1966 but had failed to deliver in office. It may well turn out that the existence of an independent intelligentsia was unimportant, and that what mattered was the opinions of civil servants and the political heavyweights – Mr Lawson,[19] Sir Geoffrey Howe, Lord Joseph and, preeminently, Mrs Thatcher herself – after the acquiescence of the last three under Mr Heath.

---

[18] Under the management of Mr Gerald Frost and Sir Alfred Sherman.
[19] Who, as editor of the *Spectator* between 1966 and 1970, had been one of the earliest critics of the prevailing economic orthodoxy.

In the early stages of her prime ministership Mrs Thatcher's achievements were negligible, her relations with her cabinets peculiar, and her leadership, at least until the Falklands War, as provisional as Gladstone's were normally. Historians will make their usual enquiries about the Civil Service, the Cabinet and the parliamentary party both then and since, and about any friends whom Mrs Thatcher may have been in the habit of consulting. They will also want to know whether the Institute of Economic Affairs and the Centre for Policy Studies (through access to Mrs Thatcher and Lord Joseph), the Prime Minister's Policy Unit (under Messrs Hoskyns, Mount, Redwood[20] and Brian Griffiths),[21] and the Conservative Research Department (once restored to doctrinal respectability by Mr Robin Harris) have supplied advice and advisers, including economic advisers, that might not have arrived by other routes if these had not been available; and whether, or to what extent, publicity advisers have established a creative connection between publicity and policy.

Powellism anticipated, Thatcherism coincided with, changes in economic opinion which occurred very generally among economists, civil servants and financial commentators of all political opinions in face of the economic decline of the 1970s. They were also parts of a struggle for power, victory in which enabled Mrs Thatcher to play radical variations on that patriotic conjunction of freedom, authority, inequality, individualism and average decency and respectability, which had been the Conservative Party's theme since at least 1886 and the aspiration it had maintained through all the resistances it had encoun-

[20] Authors of *The Theatre of Politics, The Man Who Rode Ampersand* and *The Subversive Family* etc. (Mount), *Reason, Ridicule and Religion, Public Enterprise in Crisis, Controlling Public Industries, Going for Broke* and *Equity for Everyman* etc. (Redwood).
[21] Formerly Lecturer in Economics at the London School of Economics and Professor at the City University.

tered from, and all the concessions it had made to, the higher thought, collectivist practice and the caution, or reluctance, of its leaders.

The Conservative Party under Mrs Thatcher has used a radical rhetoric to give intellectual respectability to what the Conservative Party has always wanted, and in the absence of the Labour Party, has created a cadre, like the cadres of Pitt and Peel, to which, once created, not only civil servants, politicians, entrepreneurs and conventional millionaires but also dons and journalists, from Lord Blake, Sir David English and Mr Andrew Neil at one end to Lord Dacre, Sir John Plumb and Mr Kelvin MacKenzie at the other end,[22] have found it natural, or prudent, to give support, even when they have not shared the austere conviction of Mr Congdon, the buccaneering conviction of Professor Norman Stone or the rational conviction of Mr Redwood, Mr Willetts and the younger Mr Letwin.[23] In all this Mrs Thatcher's government and the Conservative Party have had very little to do with the London School of Economics Right and virtually nothing to do with the Peterhouse Right and Professor Scruton's Right.[24]

Professor Scruton's Right consists of the authors of the *Salisbury Review* under his editorship[25] and is the nearest

[22] Sir John Plumb claims (*The Making of an Historian*, pp. 156–7) that in *Crisis in the Humanities* in 1964 he spoke 'for some elements in the suburban Conservatism which was to carry, decades later, Mrs Thatcher to power'. *Crisis in the Humanities* did not seem to be doing this at the time; on the contrary, it seemed to be a pseudo-book about a pseudo-problem, and to reflect the prudently trendy image which Sir John had seemed to be developing in the age of Mr Wilson before the rolling of the Thatcher bandwagon had suggested the desirability of a prudent conversion. For a considered view of Sir John's mind, see Cowling, *Religion and Public Doctrine in Modern England*, vol. I, pp. 376–9.
[23] Author of *Ethics, Emotion and the Unity of the Self* and *Privatisation*.
[24] Neither has it had anything to do with the Conservative Philosophy Group, founded a decade ago by Dr John Casey of Caius College, Cambridge, Professor Scruton, Sir Hugh Fraser M.P. and Mr Jonathan Aitken M.P., which, in spite of publicity to the contrary, is an exclusively *discussion* group for dons, journalists and M.P.s at which Mrs Thatcher has put in occasional appearances but which has no policies of its own and has never made any attempt to have policies.
[25] Including especially Messrs Crowther, Grant, Levy, and O'Hear. *The Salisbury Review* has owed much to Dr Casey's period as editor of the *Cambridge Review* between

intellectually reputable thing that England has had to the authoritarian Conservatism which de Maistre, in a Christian, and Maurras in a post-Christian, mode had propagated in France. It was for a time crudely anti-Marxist, is insensitive to the refractoriness of political circumstances, and has attracted special attention from the Left not only because of the unintentional caricature it sometimes provides of the ways in which Conservatives think but also because of the exaggerated importance which the Left attaches to intelligentsia politics, especially in the form of the shotgun marriage which Professor Scruton has arranged between Wittgenstein, Hegel, Kant, Oakeshott, Leavis, Eliot, Powell, Anglo-Saxon philosophy and the English Common Law.

Professor Scruton is a serious thinker who has produced a versatile and impressive oeuvre which, in addition to dealing with law and politics, deals with aesthetics, literature, philosophy and sexuality (in a sometimes off-beam way), gives unambiguous allegiance to art and culture as modern substitutes for religion,[26] and leaves the impression of believing in 'Conservatism' either as an aborted mixture of Christianity and secular truth, or as simply secular truth in itself. For a number of years when young

1975 and 1979 when, in association among others with Dr David Watkin and Mr Oliver Letwin, he laid down some of the lines which *The Salisbury Review* was to follow. *The Salisbury Review* began publication in 1982 as the organ of the Salisbury Group which had been founded by Mrs Diana Spearman and Lord Salisbury in 1978, had had its name chosen for it by Professor Oakeshott in memory of the 3rd Marquis of Salisbury, and has had on its Executive Committee at various times, among others, Mr Utley, Professor Richard Griffiths, Professor Scruton, Professor Kedourie, Sir Charles Pickthorn, the present author and Mr Richard Sykes, the libel solicitor of the *Daily* and *Sunday Telegraphs*. The Salisbury Group, like the Conservative Philosophy Group, is primarily a discussion group, has no policies of its own, and has had no discernible effect on party or governmental policy or thinking.
[26] For an explicit statement of this, see Professor Scruton's inaugural lecture at Birkbeck College, London, '*The Philosopher on Dover Beach*', reprinted in *The Times Literary Supplement*, 23 May 1986. For Professor Scruton generally, see his *Fortnight's Anger*, *Sexual Desire*, *The Meaning of Conservatism*, *The Aesthetics of Architecture*, *Art and Imagination*, *The Politics of Culture*, *Kant*, *Spinoza* and *A Short History of Modern Philosophy*.

he was a pupil and collaborator of Dr John Casey[27] from whom he acquired intellectual range and seriousness, a faint excess of high-principled intensity, and a coat-trailing, or Irish, contentiousness about race and colour which he has since abandoned. Also, when young, he was a Fellow of Peterhouse, from which he acquired some of the attitudes of 'the Peterhouse Right'.

The 'Peterhouse Right' is the name given by their critics to a small group of dons whose teaching and writing is about the history of politics, art, thought and religion, and who share a common connection with Peterhouse, the oldest and in the twentieth century one of the more admirable colleges in the University of Cambridge. Though their cohesiveness should not be exaggerated and some of them are no longer at Peterhouse, its members also share common prejudices – against the higher liberalism and all sorts of liberal rhetoric, including ecclesiastical liberal rhetoric, and in favour of irony, geniality and malice as solvents of enthusiasm, virtue and political elevation. They wish élites and establishments to eschew guilt and self-doubt, to perform the duties of their stations, and to avoid unrealistic claims about their rectitude, and they have tended to assume, ignorantly and flippantly – what Professor Vincent once stated in criticism of the Institute of Economic Affairs – that 'night-school economics', though preferable to Keynesian economics and useful in the political situation of the 1970s, are politically boring. More positively, they state that government and politics have dignities, languages and reasons of their own, that these require illusionless refurbishing in every generation, and that they should not be subordinated to even the most compatible of economic doctrines.

[27] Fellow of Gonville and Caius College, Cambridge, and Lecturer in English in the University. Author of *The Language of Criticism* and (ed.) *Morality and Moral Reasoning*. For an account of Dr Casey's opinions, see Charles Covell, *The Redefinition of Conservatism* pp. 15–42.

Dr Watkin,[28] Professor Vincent, Dr Jonathan Clark, the present author and Dr Norman[29] believe in 'Conservatism' as secular truth as little as they believe in 'Liberalism' or 'Socialism' as secular truth, and they accompany distaste for 'secular truth' with the belief, whether issuing in religious observance or not, that 'secular truth' tends to be solemn and that secular truths tend to the dissolution of Christianity.

The Peterhouse Right is mistrustful of higher education as it has developed in Britain in the last twenty-five years, believes that if higher education is to be extensive, it should educate practical capabilities, and wishes that the Robbins expansion could have been vocational and technological.[30] It also believes that the sort of education which British universities have provided since the middle of the nineteenth century is valuable, in the sciences as well as in the humanities – provided that there is a lot less of it than there is at present – and that the tendency of Mrs Thatcher's government to be interested mainly in the financial aspects of higher education and to blame universities for difficulties which were caused by the Home government's acceptance of the Robbins Report, is obscuring the fact that this sort of education *is* valuable.

The Peterhouse Right is an academic Right – a set of monastic, or country, cousins who have some journalistic connections and weak political connections, and whose chief practical success has been the election of Lord Dacre to the Mastership of Peterhouse,[31] not so much on the

[28] Author, among many other books, of *Morality and Architecture*, *A History of Western Architecture*, *German Architecture and the Classical Idea*, *The English Vision*, (with Montgomery–Massingberd) *The London Ritz*, *Thomas Hope and the Neo-Classical Ideal* and *Peterhouse: An Architectural Record 1284–1984*.
[29] Author, again among very many other books, of *Church and Society in England 1770–1970* and *Christianity and the World Order*.
[30] In the sense in which, for all his over-emphases, Mr Corelli Barnett means it.
[31] Lord Dacre has written an article ('The Cambridge Connection' in *The Sunday Telegraph* of 26 March 1989) which describes the 'neo-Toryism of the 1980s' as being not only 'Cambridge-fed' but also a 'grim and doctrinaire' continuation of the

ground that he was the best candidate – such a consideration seldom operating in elections of this sort – as on the
ironical, genial or malicious grounds that, in the circumstances in which he ws being elected, he was the candidate
most likely to serve everyone right.

The Peterhouse Right includes only a small number of
the Fellows of Peterhouse, amongst whom there is solid
worth and scientific distinction; but a number of the
journalists and publicists of the New Right have been
undergraduates, graduates or fellows of the college[32] and
Mrs Letwin was an unbeneficed teacher for a number of
years after her resignation from the London School of
Economics in the 1970s.

Between the Peterhouse Right and the London School

'Cambridge puritanism' of the seventeenth century. Lord Dacre obviously dislikes both
the 'Peterhouse Right' and the 'neo-Toryism of the 1980s'. In fact, with one possible
exception, no member of either could reasonably be thought of as 'puritan'. In both
there is a strong streak of sceptical satire, both about Lord Dacre himself and about the
egalitarianism of his Oxford friends, Sir A. Ayer, Sir I. Berlin and Sir S. Hampshire.
The idea of the neo-Toryism of the 1980s being 'puritan' rises into farce when applied
to Professor Norman Stone (see p. oo above) who, until he became Professor of Modern
History at Oxford, had spent his adult life in Cambridge, and though not part of the
'Peterhouse Right', was certainly a 'Cambridge neo-Tory of the 1980s'.

In 'teaching' his 'tale' of the Peterhouse Right, Lord Dacre has become an *Ancient
Mariner*, though clubmen in London, journalists on the Isle of Dogs, colleagues in the
House of Lords, hosts in American universities and innocent fellows of Oxford and
Cambridge Colleges must wonder why it so so necessary to slay the birds that made his
breeze to blow.

[32] In addition to Professor Scruton, Professor Vincent, Dr Watkin, Dr Norman, Dr
Jonathan Clark and the present author, who are now, or have at various times been
Fellows of Peterhouse, the following who appear in this introduction have been either
undergraduates or research students of the college – Mr Gale, Mr Peter Fuller, Dr
Andrew Jones, Dr Patrick Cosgrave, the official biographer of Mr Powell and the first
journalist to predict Mrs Thatcher's victory over Mr Heath in 1975, and Mr Welch
and Mr Worsthorne, who came from Stowe School to Peterhouse together and were
later to be on the staff of *The Daily Telegraph* together. It is of no significance that Dr
Noel Malcolm, the present political correspondent of *The Spectator*, read history at
Peterhouse and that Dr Caroline Moore, the wife of Mr Charles Moore, the present
editor of *The Spectator*, is Peterhouse's first woman Fellow. Dr Moore is a literary critic
or historian rather than a politician and Dr Malcom, though endowed, like Mr Moore,
with Conservative sympathies, holds them in the diffident and unenthusiastic way of an
intelligent and unusually learned, but acreless, Etonian. In any case the *Spectator*
maintains under Mr Moore, as it generally has under previous editors, except during
Mr Gale's anti-European and virtually Powellite editorship in the early 1970s, a far
blander position than a 'New Right' label might suggest.

of Economics Right, there are affinities, the latter, in the persons of Dr Charvet, Dr Beattie and Professor and Mrs Letwin, being enemies of collectivism and liberal certainty,[33] Professor Minogue having an Oakeshottian hatred of 'ideological shibboleths' and 'the liberal mind',[34] and Professor Kedourie, with whom the anti-secular affinity is strongest,[35] presenting the secular problem in a Muslim and Jewish as well as in a Christian framework.

Professor Scruton's Right, the Peterhouse Right and the London School of Economics Right have all had some effect on the opinions which seep outwards from the universities. Dr Watkin was an early contributor to the by now established attack on architectural modernism. Professor Scruton has a following in schools, polytechnics and universities and even, oddly, among the Conservative clergy. Dr Norman was the first satirist of Synodical government in the Church of England and the first postwar writer effectively to suggest that the Bench of Bishops was both objectionably liberal in its theology and objectionably collectivist in its politics. And it is also the case that these three, together with Mrs Letwin, Professor Kedourie, Minogue and Vincent, and now Dr Jonathan Clark, have all had periods as productive journalists or book-reviewers, including in Professor Vincent's case an eventful period as a political columnist for *The Sun*.

[33] For liberal certainty see Shirley Letwin, *The Pursuit of Certainty*. For libertarian statements see her essay 'On Conservative Individualism' in *Conservative Essays*, John Charvet, *A Critique of Freedom and Equality*, W. Letwin, *On the Study of Public Policy, Law and Economic Policy in America*, *The Origins of Economic Science* and (ed.) *Against Equality* (including essays by Charvet, Bauer, Tulloch, etc. etc.) Mrs Letwin and Professor Minogue are members of the Board of Directors of the Centre for Policy Studies, though it is doubtful whether that indicates much more than a general sympathy with some aspects of Conservative policy since 1979.

[34] For 'the liberal mind' see especially Kenneth Monogue, *The Liberal Mind*. For Minogue generally see also *Nationalism, The Concept of a University, Alien Powers*, etc.

[35] For the anti-secular position in Kedourie see especially E. Kedourie, *Nationalism, Nationalism in Asia and Africa, The Chatham House Version* and *Islam in the Modern World*. For Kedourie generally see *England and the Middle East, Afghani and Abduh, The Chatham House Version, The Crossman Confessions, Diamonds into Glass* etc. etc.

Where public opinion is concerned, nevertheless, it is the professional journalists who have been of first importance.

In this connection, 'New Right' may be a misnomer, since some of the journalists concerned grew up in the shadow of Butterfield, Brogan, Oakeshott and *The Cambridge Journal*,[36] and were surprised when the opinions they had picked up in the 1940s and 1950s became acceptable in the 1970s and 1980s. Neither would a later generation have been given their heads if Mr Maurice Green, as editor of *The Daily Telegraph* from 1964 onwards and a long-standing believer in market economics, had not appointed as his deputy editor Mr Colin Welch, one of the most intelligent of Conservative journalists and also a long-standing believer in market economics, or if, after Mr Welch had brought Mr T. E. Utley on to the paper and they between them had brought on Mr John O'Sullivan and Mr Frank Johnson, Lord Deedes had suppressed them when he in his turn became editor in the problematical situation of 1974.

For *The Daily Telegraph* to be a free-market newspaper was nothing new. What was new was that through Welch, Utley, O'Sullivan and Johnson, and through Mr Michael Wharton as *Peter Simple*,[37] an old dog bared new teeth at old enemies, and that Welch's Hayekianism, Utley's High Toryism, Johnson's and Wharton's satire, and O'Sullivan's political engagements, were pointed at Mr Heath as Conservative leader, particularly after he had ceased

[36] Which was founded by one of the silent props of post-war English intellectual Conservatism, Professor Desmond Williams of University College, Dublin, while a research student of Sir Herbert Butterfield at Peterhouse in 1948.

[37] Authors of *Enoch Powell, Edmund Burke* and *Lessons of Ulster* (Utley), *Out of Order* and *Frank Johnson's Election Year* (Johnson) and *Peter Simple, Way of the World, Peter Simple in Opposition, The Thoughts of Peter Simple* and *The Best of Peter Simple* (Wharton). Johnson and O'Sullivan had a lot to do with Lord Joseph when the Centre for Policy Studies was being formed in the period immediately before and after the fall of Mr Heath. They, and Mr Utley, also had a certain amount to do with Mrs Thatcher at the same time.

to be prime minister, with greater subtlety, intelligence and information than even well-informed Conservative newspapers are normally able to point at Conservative leaders.

The transformation in the stature of *The Daily Telegraph*, though followed by the departure of Utley, Johnson and O'Sullivan to *The Times*, is the most striking incident in the process we are discussing, predating Lord Rees-Mogg's conversion[38] while editor of *The Times*, the encouragement given by Mr Charles Douglas-Home to market economics, Cold Warriordom and the New Right after Mr Murdoch's purchase of *The Times* in the early 1980s, and the demonstrations given, continuously by the *Daily* and *Sunday Express*, less continuously by *The Economist*, *The Financial Times*, *The Daily Mail* and *The Sunday Times*, during the 1980s. Mr Worsthorne has been chief political correspondent of *The Sunday Telegraph* since it was founded in 1961; one of the most confident and pleasing realisations of the journalistic New Right has been the upmarket demonstration he gave as editor of *The Sunday Telegraph* between 1986 and 1989, when political precision, Chestertonian paradox and an Oakeshottian contempt for the liberal intelligentsia, along with regular contributions from Mr Auberon Waugh, Lord Harris, Lord Bruce-Gardyne, Mr Fuller, Dr Norman, Mr Powell, Mr Bruce Anderson, Mr Frank Johnson, Professor Scruton, Dr Casey and Dr Jonathan Clark, created as admirable a conjunction of confirmation and critical invigilation as could be expected in a Conservative newspaper of Mrs Thatcher, the economic New Right and the aims and assumptions of suburban Conservatism.[39]

[38] For Lord Rees-Mogg's conversion, see *The Reigning Error: The Crisis of World Inflation* and *Democracy and the Value of Money*.
[39] For Mr Worsthorne as author see *The Socialist Myth* (1971) and *Peregrinations* (1980). For recent examples of Mr Worsthorne's best manner see 'The Blooding of the Literati' and 'War on the Professions' in *The Sunday Telegraph*, 19 February and 5 March 1989.

The cumulative effect of the journalistic transformation has been considerable.[40] It has eased Mrs Thatcher's way with Conservative electors and the Conservative Party, has persuaded the Conservative thinking classes that the weight of the argument is on their side, and has turned against the Left the assumption which the satire of the late 1960s had turned against the Right – that politics can properly be considered as farce, or, indeed, in *The Sun*, as pornography.

The journalism of the New Right has registered, and helped to create, a significant change in public thought, though only Utley, Mount, O'Sullivan, Anderson, Sherman, Bruce-Gardyne and Cosgrave, among the professional journalists, have had experience of government or the management of the Conservative Party. But really everyone agrees, apart possibly in their differing ways from Scruton, Casey and Sherman, that, though doctrine matters, the Conservative Party should not wish to be either doctrinaire or authoritarian.

(iii)

What have been described are five overlapping movements, conducted by about fifty people (mainly graduates and mostly men) who have come from no one type of social, sexual or intellectual background and who include among their number a smattering of atheists and agnostics, a few converted, a few practising and a few lapsed Catholics, a handful of Jews, observing or otherwise, some Dissenters and Evangelicals, a fair number of observing and a number of converted Anglicans, and a contingent for whom religion is of little significance.

[40] However little the managers, and even the journalists, of the *Telegraphs* believe that the opinions which they were promoting had any significant impact on their readers.

In opinion there has been a lack of stereotype. Many of those who have supported market economics have been authoritarian about moral and social questions, many who supported Mr Powell economically did not support him about Europe, Ireland, Immigration or the Soviet Union. Cold Warriors and anti-Cold Warriors, Europeans and anti-Europeans, Americans and anti-Americans, and both the friends and the enemies of Israel, have been distributed fairly randomly. Some of the economists – Mr Samuel Brittan, for example – have come to be unenthusiastic about Mrs Thatcher, among whose most enthusiastic supporters are ex-Socialists some of whom assume that society can be reformed by legislation. Sir John Junor, Mr Brian Walden and Mr Ronald Spark, the chief leader-writer of *The Sun*, are Thatcherites without being Conservatives, and there are signs, chiefly in *The Sun*, of a Thatcherite anti-establishmentarianism which does not spare the monarchy. Messrs Alexander, Welch, Biffen, Cosgrave, Butt, Gale, O'Sullivan, Frank Johnson, and others who would find it embarrassing to be mentioned, were admirers of Mr Powell before they settled for Mrs Thatcher. Mr Utley, intellectually the most impregnable of Conservatives, while moving from being a Butlerian in the 1950s through being a Powellite in the 1960s to being a speechwriter for Mrs Thatcher in the 1980s, insisted, with reservations in the cases of both Mr Powell and Mrs Thatcher, that all three were exponents of an undoctrinaire traditional Conservatism with which the economic movement need not be in conflict, provided it was kept out of the hands of the bigots. Even Mr Worsthorne, whose emphasis has been on the duties of ruling classes during nearly thirty years on *The Sunday Telegraph*, has combined distaste for Mrs Thatcher's *persona* with approval of many of the changes which she has effected.

Like Mr Waugh, who has also occupied a leading place in *The Sunday Telegraph*, Mr Worsthorne is an upper-class Catholic or lapsed Catholic Tory who feels no need to prove himself socially. Others, feeling the need, have become snobs or élitists, have adopted the affectation of holding all élites in contempt, or have found in Mrs Thatcher's 'classless Conservatism' a relief from the upper-class, public-school, metropolitan tone of the Conservative Party as it was before her. However subdued the sexual consideration and however difficult the religious consideration once the Church of England became hooked onto the politics of the day-before-yesterday, there can be no doubt that the upper reaches of the Conservative Party during the last decade have witnessed a discreetly conducted and unresolved class war which has centred around the mentality of the grammar schools of the 1940s and 1950s, the assumptions and resentments of secularized dissent, and the sense of exclusion which made many lower-middle-class intellectuals stalwarts of Socialism between the wars.

The sexual, religious and social considerations operate in complicated ways and are sometimes difficult to trace. Political conversions are less difficult to trace and may be the more important since the idea of a political Broad Church attracting converts may well have been in Mrs Thatcher's and Lord Joseph's minds from the start. Certainly conversions of one sort or another have been numerous. Professor Minogue, for example, was a student Marxist in Australia in the 1950s, Professor Vincent an activist of the Left in England in the 1960s, and the late Lord Vaizey, the economist, a Labour City Councillor who had toyed with Lord Grimond's Liberal Party before eventually becoming a Thatcherite life peer. Sir Alfred Sherman was a Marxist volunteer in the Spanish Civil War before moving via Mr Welch and *The Daily Telegraph* to Lord Joseph and Mrs Thatcher, Mr Bruce Anderson was both a student Trotskyite and a follower of Sir Ian Gilmour before becoming the intellectual hard-liner of *The Sunday Telegraph*, and Mr Rupert Murdoch was an active member of the Oxford University Labour Club and a supporter of the Australian Labour Party before turning *The Sun* into an organ of working-class Thatcherism. Mr Paul Johnson[41] and Lord Wyatt have been the most loyal of Mrs Thatcher's journalistic protectors in the 1980s; the one had been editor of the *New Statesman* before becoming a prolific historian, the other had been a Labour M.P., Parliamentary Private Secretary to Sir Stafford Cripps, and a junior Labour minister before becoming a Thatcherite life peer and Mrs Thatcher's Chairman of the Horse Race Totalisator Board. Sir Alan Walters[42] and Lord Young, two of Mrs Thatcher's more prominent advisers, were originally Labour voters and Sir Rhodes Boyson a Labour Councillor. Lord Thomas,[43] the present Chairman of the Centre for Policy Studies, having been a Conservative President of the Union at Cambridge, wrote an anti-Foreign Office novel after a short period in the Foreign Office in the 1950s and was a Labour parliamentary candidate in a hopeless constituency before spending a successful and productive decade as Professor of History at Reading. Baroness Cox was a sociologist, a Socialist and a nurse before being turned by experience of lecturing at the North London Polytechnic into a Conservative Baroness-in-Waiting and Deputy Speaker of the House of

[41] Author of *The Suez War*, *Journey into Chaos*, *Left of Centre*, *Statesmen and Nations*, *The Offshore Islanders*, (with George Gale) *The Highland Jaunt*, *Pope John XXIII*, *A History of Christianity*, *Enemies of Society*, *The Recovery of Freedom*, *A History of the Modern World*, *A History of the Jews*, etc. etc.
[42] Author of (with Clower and Dalton) *Growth Without Development*, *Economics of Road User Charges*, *An Introduction to Econometrics*, *Money in Boom and Slump*, (with Layard) *Micro-Economic Theory*, *Britain's Economic Renaissance*, etc. etc.
[43] Author of *The World's Game*, *The Spanish Civil War*, *The Suez Affair*, *Cuba*, *Europe the Radical Challenge*, *John Strachey*, *The Cuban Revolution*, *An Unfinished History of the World*, *Armed Truce*, etc. etc.

Lords. Skeletons also rattle in the cupboards of Lord Beloff, Professor Julius Gould, Sir Reginald Prentice and many others besides. The present author has no skeletons in his cupboard, but he certainly said, and probably believed, in the late 1960s that, if the revolting students of the Student Revolution were revolting against Lord Beloff, Lord Annan and Sir Isaiah Berlin, there must have been *something* to be said in their favour.

During Mrs Thatcher's prime ministership there have been important changes in credit policy, prices and income policy and taxation policy, in television and broadcasting, exchange control, council-house and privatisation policy, and in governmental attitudes to the professions, unemployment, and the trade unions, as a result of which politicians of all parties have felt obliged to agree that Mrs Thatcher has rewritten their agenda.

The remarkable nature of Mrs Thatcher's achievement is not in doubt, but many things in politics are not what they seem and many changes which seem to have happened turn out on investigation not to have happened. Collectivism, socialism and the higher liberalism have not gone away, politically or intellectually. Their advocates are taking a long time to regroup but they *are* regrouping, waiting for Mrs Thatcher to retire or be beaten, or judging that it is not necessary to wait for her to retire or be beaten. It would be wrong to claim more than limited gains and a rhetorical ascendancy for the uncoordinated conjunction of libertarianism and authoritarianism, scepticism and belief, doctrine and resistance to doctrine, high culture and dislike of high culture, economic truth and disdain for economic truth, which, under conflicting guidance from Hayek, Oakeshott, Butterfield, Leavis, Eliot, Powell and Mrs Thatcher, has constituted the New Right of the last twenty-five years.

The 'New Right', in other words, has been moving in

divergent directions which have converged on the belief that there should in some sense be less government rather than more, even if at times on the way this involves more government rather than less. But the change has been marginal and the explanatory assumptions unrelated to it.

Hayekian (and Friedmanite) assumptions may be admirable economically; politically they are wooden, indifferent to countervailing knowledge, and insensitive to the fact that inherited luggage cannot be abandoned. Whatever is needed in practice, what is needed in theory is a response to facts, including the facts of class and belief, and rejection of the idea that models of conduct can properly ignore them. The Institute of Economic Affairs, the economic movement and the Hayekian model have had a tactical use as antidotes to Keynesianism, as justifications for Capitalism, and as proof that the Conservative Party is a thinking party. The result, however, has been a government of financial stringency and administrative reform which, though exactly what was needed at the beginning of the 1980s, has provided no resolution of the contradiction between the diminution of the scope of government through financial stringency and administrative reform, and the increases which financial stringency and administrative reform have wrought in the scope of government.

The Conservative Party is not especially innovative, is not instinctively meritocratic even now, and expresses itself in defensive idioms – about inequality and its preservation, about the crucial nature of the difference between compassion and sentimentality, and about national identity, the dignity of state power and law and foreign policy as its primary areas of operation. In these respects, though Oakeshott is better than Hayek, neither conceptualises the mixture of politeness and negative bloodiness which is the antidote to liberal virtue.

Negative bloodiness is not an end in itself but is instrumental to the assertion of a conservative moral order which needs active assertion when threatened by liberal insinuation. It is a temperamental as much as an intellectual characteristic and requires a tone and posture as much as it requires an argument. The innovative ideas of the last decade have been justified in terms of the prosperity they will bring and the disasters they will avoid. Their best justification is this temperamental negativity which is needed everywhere – not just in the political parties but throughout the thinking classes, and as much now as at any time in the past.

In the past decade it has been easy to identify the threat from socialist virtue. It has been less easy to identify the threat from liberal virtue. Moreover, in spite of the vigour of Mrs Thatcher's personality and much intelligent day-to-day anticipation, there has been only a low-level, Neville Chamberlain-type conception of the spiritual glue which is one of the Conservative Party's special needs.

The absence of glue has not mattered since 1975, when Labour misjudgments, Mr Foot's election as leader of the Labour Party, and Mr Benn's assumption of the leadership of the student revolution, have destroyed the consensual attractions from which the Labour Party had benefited under Attlee. These temporary advantages have been made more permanent by both luck and judgment and may be made more permanent still by luck and judgment in the future. The time may come, however – it may have come already – when luck will run out and glue will be in short supply.

It is always desirable to mistrust intelligentsia politics, especially when a nostrum provides a specifick against the future. At the same time the business of the Conservative Party is to win elections or, by its impregnability, to prevent too much damage being done when elections are lost, and in both situations it needs reserves of belief which can be called up without having to be created on each particular occasion. In calling belief up, relating it to the requirements of situations and creating further belief in their turn, politicians are paramount. The forms and sources of belief, however, are numerous, and though not to be found amongst the Conservative intelligentsia alone, *are* to be found there, even when the intelligentsia's perception of timing and suitability cut across politicians' perceptions of timing and suitability, and the disjunction between them creates the impression that the Conservative Party is 'anti-intellectual', when in fact Conservative 'anti-intellectualism' has for over a hundred years been merely one aspect of a subtle, multi-faced highly intellectual body of assumptions about the duties of the rich and the educated, and about the nature and powers of the State, which will need to be given new twists if the Conservative Party is to negotiate its way through the coming decade.

Like *Mill and Liberalism*, this introduction is a contribution to Conservative belief, to Conservative anti-intellectualism in this sense, and to the reserves of eloquence which the Conservative Party requires in order to propagate belief. Its message is that eloquence is complementary to the cynicism of democratic politics, that democratic eloquence is capable of being Conservative, and, as Mrs Thatcher is perfectly well able to demonstrate, that the eloquence of Hayek and Adam Smith is not enough.

This, proleptically, is the context in which *Mill and Liberalism* should be placed. It was Conservative by sympathy and disposition but, so far from being doctrinaire, demanded a non-doctrinaire mentality – a negative reaction which combined an anti-liberal defence of authority with a vigorous defence of liberty against 'the

tyranny of liberalism'. Written before the Marxist movement of the 1970s and the Thatcher governments of the
1980s, it did not envisage either the sociological significance of what it was saying or the narrowing toughness
which the Conservative Party would have to take on
board before a Conservative conception of authority
could be made credible. All it saw, but what it saw very
clearly, was that it did not wish the existing orthodoxy to
be perpetuated.

In the early 1960s the author, though better equipped
to be a don, still hoped to be a politician, and shuffled
between denying the connection between 'political' and
'academic' and giving an arbitrary content to the connection. As it became obvious that he both ought to be, and
would have to be, a don, he came increasingly to understand that the contrast between political and academic is
academic, that dons play a part, however obscurely, in
the development of the public mind, and that the way in
which they do this is through teaching and writing, by
informing teaching and writing with a tone and a posture,
and by avoiding the claim to be 'statesmen in disguise'.

This may sound like a claim that universities are
guardians of high political culture. Nothing could be
farther from the author's intention. *Mill and Liberalism* was
anti-Arnoldian, and believed on the one hand that the
nation's political future was in the hands of its politicians
and on the other hand that popular instincts should be
respected, not only because it is prudent to respect them
in a democratic system, but also because there is duty to
do so, where possible, in the interest of a necessary moral
cohesion.

Is *Mill and Liberalism* worth reading twenty-five years
after it was published? That is something for the reader to
judge. What the author can say is that the political and
intellectual climates have moved in the direction he

wished them to move in when he wrote it, that he is conscious now of a more congenial climate than he was conscious of in 1963, and that *Mill and Liberalism* speaks congenially to him, not just because it willed guilt, collectivism and the higher liberalism to go away, but because it believed that party, parliament, and public opinion could be relied on to make them do so.

In a review of *Mill and Liberalism* in 1964, a reviewer in *Sanity*, the organ of the Campaign for Nuclear Disarmament, wrote that any nuclear disarmer who was accustomed to talking about 'values, moral decision ... and advantaging mankind in general ... should read this book'.[44] The Campaign for Nuclear Disarmament was then, as it is now, a party of virtue, so it is unlikely that the reviewer's advice was taken. But the advice had its point and so completely retains its point in the age of the welfare worker, the liberal bishop, the race-relations and third-world industries, and the counter-cultures embodied in the Green movement, the Feminist movement and the rag-bag of movements which hang around Mr Kenneth Livingstone that, quite apart from any significance which *Mill and Liberalism* may have for the interpretation of Mill himself, it is because its tone and posture are well suited to absorbing, outsmarting and seeing off whatever the parties of virtue, including the parties of civic and bureaucratic virtue,[45] come up with in the 1990s that the author has agreed that this unrevised reprint should be offered to the public.

MAURICE COWLING

PETERHOUSE

CAMBRIDGE

44 Tony McCarthy, 'Satanic Mill', in *Sanity*, January 1964.
45 Bureaucratic virtue tends to be surreptitious; for a pious statement of civic virtue see Q. R. D. Skinner, 'The Parodox of Political Liberty' in ed. S. McMurrin *The Tanner Lectures on Human Values*, 1986.

xlv

INTRODUCTION

Each generation of scholars, and within each generation each group, takes the past left by its predecessors, makes what alteration it thinks it can justify, and constructs for itself a world from which it has emerged. This process occurs over all areas of scholarly activity: it occurs over all areas of history: it occurs, more even than elsewhere, in interpreting writers whom earlier generations have chosen, for reasons as various as their experiences, to regard as 'great moral teachers'.

This process must be carried out by each generation for itself. It cannot be done for it by the generation before, and it cannot be done by the generation after. Their experiences are different from its own: the weight of their emphasis will be different also. It can be done only by those who are in some sense contemporary, and there is no other way of doing it than by studying the texts. Not everyone will recognize the experience of the author by whom this book is written: but some will understand the hostility to Mill which arises from suspicion of the claim to impartiality, rationality and unquestionable self-evidence with which liberal opinions and progressive policies have been propagated through all political parties, and most political journals, in the eighteen years which have elapsed since the end of the war of 1939. In another work[1] the author has set out objections to the academic predominance of this style of thinking: the present work is a continuation of that one.

[1] Maurice Cowling, *The Nature and Limits of Political Science*, Cambridge 1963.

The *life* of John Stuart Mill has, over the last eighteen years, been subjected to intensive investigation. It is too early to say yet that we have all the material necessary to understand his character: but the material presented by Professors Mueller, von Hayek and Rees, and by Mr Packe, has extended the picture we had before. Further definition will depend on detailed biographical investigation, and this book is not a contribution to that. Mill has, also, as a repository of liberal truths, received of late (as he always has done since he wrote) a good deal of attention from the various sorts of political moralist. Most of this attention has been respectful: it has not all been superficial; but much of it suffers the limitations of its scope. It uses Mill's writing as a body of scripture or collection of texts; so long as the texts support the position his authority is used to justify, it matters little whether they performed the same function in Mill's writings as they perform in the writings of Professor MacKinnon or the late Sir Ernest Barker.

Justification for another book on Mill will be found, therefore, if justification is needed, on three lines. It will be found, first, in the fact that the account given here of Mill's doctrine differs from the account assumed by most modern interpreters. Mill, the godfather of English liberalism, emerges from these pages considerably less libertarian than is sometimes suggested.[2] He emerges considerably more radical, and, without straining words unduly, may be accused of more than a touch of something resembling moral totalitarianism. His emphasis on social cohesion and moral consensus at all periods of his life was of the greatest consequence; whilst commitment to elevate character and make moral reasoning self-critical leaves less room for variegated human development than

[2] By, e.g., Professor R. P. Anschutz, *The Philosophy of J. S. Mill*, Oxford 1953, and Professor Karl Britton, *John Stuart Mill*, London 1953.

some writers have imagined. Because his opinions have
become part of a prevailing orthodoxy, their aggressive-
ness is less obvious than when he wrote: because they
express, even in victory, disarming intentions of universal
benevolence, they are often taken to be more comprehensive than they were. Mill's doctrine was liberal: but his
liberalism was neither comprehensive nor libertarian: it
attempted dogmatically to erode the assumptions on
which competing doctrines were based. One competing
doctrine was Christianity: in Mill's hands, Liberalism was
not compatible with it. Liberalism, no less than Marxism,
is intolerant of competition: jealousy, and a carefully
disguised intolerance, are important features of Mill's
intellectual personality.

On Liberty, therefore, has been one of the most influential of modern political tracts chiefly, on this view,
because its purpose has been misunderstood. *On Liberty*,
contrary to common opinion, was not so much a plea for
individual freedom, as a means of ensuring that Christianity would be superseded by that form of liberal, rationalistic utilitarianism which went by the name of the Religion
of Humanity. Mill's liberalism was a dogmatic, religious
one, not the soothing night-comforter for which it is
sometimes mistaken. Mill's object was not to free men, but
to convert them, and convert them to a peculiarly exclusive, peculiarly insinuating moral doctrine. Mill wished to
moralize all social activity—religion and art no less than
politics and education—and to mark each with his own
emphatic imprint. Over the last two centuries erosion of
Christendom has been a European, not just an English,
phenomenon; but it has been English nevertheless: Mill,
no less than Marx, Nietzsche or Comte, claimed to
replace Christianity by 'something better'. Atheists and
agnostics, humanists and free-thinkers may properly give
thanks to Mill. He, with Lord Russell and Matthew

il

Arnold, *is*, in England, their great tradition; irony is not involved in calling on him.

The impact of Mill, however, has not been on them alone. Over the last sixty years, innumerable public figures who would have deplored Mill's religion if they had understood it and whose purposes had nothing in common with his, have used Mill's language in order to leave the impression that they have. To use liberal language has been taken to be *intelligent*: to reject it evidence of *stupidity*. And it has been the language which has mattered, and been remembered, whilst the object to which Mill put it has been lost. Few politicians, except the greatest, are free to choose the slogans in which they speak: most have to be content with slogans that come to hand. To use slogans that happen to be current is not necessarily bad; this book does not urge politicians to renovate their slogans. Nor, so long as political objectives are achieved, do politicians need to recognize their slogans when they use them. To know that a slogan is being used, and use it as though it were something more, requires a fine combination of political instincts. In democratic societies slogans are as necessary as anywhere else: instincts of this kind are difficult to acquire: no politician is obliged to acquire them. Nevertheless, slogans, if necessary, are effective so far as they seem self-evident. Agreement about them is rare: those who dislike particular ones cannot fail, when obliged to use them, to know them for what they are. Some politicians manipulate them as tools of the trade, but not all. One slogan is used rather than another, not just according to moral conviction, but according to the chances of the political game. The chances of the political game make strange bedfellows. The body of the old Liberal Party was Christian and non-conforming in general temper, but used Mill's slogans notwithstanding. Nor is it clear how much

1

of the socially respectable, theologically committed Christian conservative *bloc*, which offers Mill's slogans as liberal conservatism today, has any understanding of the irony involved in the use to which it puts them.

Justification will be found, secondly, in the fact that the political manner of which Mill was the most powerful nineteenth-century propagator, still permeates the thinking, not only of the more liberal-minded English politician, but also of the more liberal-minded political don. This book is not a contribution to English politics: it is designed to assist understanding of Mill by developing the implications of criticism[3] which the victory of Mill's manner, in England, at least, and in relation to his own work, has silenced since the decade in which he died. Mill's confusions, however, are contemporary academic ones, and this book has an academic purpose. The academic purpose emerges through consideration of the status of what may be called *general reasoning*. Mill's social, religious and political writings are reasoning of this kind. General reasoning, though sometimes supposed to be, is not, in fact, an academic activity. It is, on the contrary, the characteristic preoccupation of the 'intelligentsia'. The 'intellectual' is distinguished from the scholar, as he is from the body of the clergy and most politicians, by the indeterminate character of his responsibility, activity or subject-matter, and by the generality of the expectations he entertains about it. In England, general reasoning is at its best, and crispest, in the higher journalism, but has had more general impact besides. Religious, economic and political life, over the last hundred years, have gained something from it. *Fabian Essays* and *The Unservile State* in this respect may be put on the same shelf as *The Humanist Frame, Lux Mundi, Foundations* or *Essays and Reviews*: and

---

[3] As made, for example, by Sir F. J. Stephen in *Liberty, Equality, Fraternity* (1873) though Stephen's assumptions were both liberal and philosophically untransparent.

the volume of this kind of contribution seems unlikely to diminish. However, if its volume is unlikely to diminish, it will be interesting to see it for what it is. Doctrinal articulation is not more necessary to the body politic than theological articulation to the Church. Both matter, but neither matters as much as the intelligentsia often tends to imagine. Habit and conduct are as significant as articulated reasoning, and seldom yield exactly to its precepts. It matters that general reasoning, if it is to be conducted, should be good, but it matters at least as much that the vast mass of less articulate persons at all levels of the national life should, in whatever ways *they* find suitable, be good also.

Nor does generality of manner guarantee knowledge of society-as-a-whole. Sometimes, indeed, the intelligentsia seems to know about *society-as-a-whole* a good deal less than other people. No one knows less than someone who thinks his knowledge is greater than it is. The obligation to write generally about matters which do not occur generally presents temptations: advice becomes blurred as explanation becomes vague. In some circumstances this does not matter. General reasons are general reasons, and slogans, slogans: the authority of neither rests on *particular* applications; nor is it necessary that it should. General reasoning involves exchange of slogans: the authority of both is the authority of those who utter them. General reasoning persuades so far as general reasoners can make it: one way of making it is to claim philosophical authority. Philosophy, however, has no time for general reasoning except to explain that it has no time for it. To suppose that general reasoning *is* philosophy is a serious philosophical error, which, when made crudely, may be rejected crudely. Mill makes it, but not crudely: his justification is bold and intelligent. Book VI of *A System of Logic* is a systematic justification of the authority of

General Sociology. Elsewhere Mill presents the intelligentsia as the guardian of general reasoning: his defence of the 'clerisy' is a defence of both. Mill's view is not now dominant everywhere, but since, in some academic quarters, its prestige remains as great as ever, and since Mill's assumptions about the intelligentsia have been shared, over the last hundred years, by those who have rejected his philosophical position as often as by those who have shared it, they receive consideration here.

Justification for this book will be found, finally, in the fact that the author himself, after expounding the salient features of Mill's doctrine, assesses the validity of Mill's views about questions of such perennial philosophical interest as the validation of a political theory, the nature and purpose of sociology, the justification of religious commitments. Religion, education, history and sociology are central to Mill's political doctrine, central to his view of the intelligentsia, and integral to the criticisms here made of it. Mill, in the last section of the book, is subjected to an attempt at critical deflation. Critically to deflate a writer who wrote a hundred years ago in a situation different from one's own is to risk deflating by historical misunderstanding. The preoccupations of the present writer, and the deflections which arise from his situation, are different from the preoccupations and deflections of Mill. They are, however, not *so* different that criticism is impossible: once the attempt has been made to understand what Mill was doing, it is legitimate to ask what validity his doctrine has. The conclusion to which investigation is brought is that Mill was a remarkably coherent, remarkably self-opinionated moral teacher, the consistency of whose practical doctrine and certainty of whose moral posture were achieved, and could in a sense only be achieved, at the price of fundamental sociological self-deception.

PART I

EXPOSITION

CHAPTER I

THE HISTORIC MISSION

The purpose of this book, then, is not to expose the development of Mill's mind, but to explain the nature of his doctrine. It will be a critical essay in the exposition of ideas, not a regurgitation of the *Autobiography*. Nevertheless, it is necessary to understand not just the doctrine, but the circumstances to which the doctrine was a response. This is a preliminary essential in dealing with all serious writers on moral, political and social questions (though often the material has to be inferred): with Mill it is central to the doctrine itself. There is about Mill at all stages of his intellectual development a sense of historic mission which gives greater confidence than he might have otherwise had, and induces an earnestness of manner deriving from consciousness of obligation to propagate what he conceived to be opinions suitable to the time and point-in-history at which he had arrived. In few nineteenth-century writers (except Marx) is this sense of historic mission as strong as in Mill: in few writers does interpretation of history so completely dominate the fundamental assumptions about the function of philosophical doctrine.

For Mill supposed, as many writers before and since have supposed, that he was living in a critical phase in the history of the world, a transitional period in which old opinions, old institutions, and the old religion were disintegrating (in most cases clearly disintegrating), and where the task of the mature, reasonable writer and mature reasonable philosopher was provision of a body of received doctrine to supply the want caused by this disintegration. The world Mill saw (which was not necessarily the world that existed around him) was a world in which the shells of old institutions continued to survive, but where the principles from which they had initially drawn their justification had departed. It is not always clear when this period of 'unfixed opinions' and decaying order had begun: but that it had begun there was in Mill's mind no doubt.

Where [he asks in 1831] is the authority which commands . . . confidence or deserves it. . . . At all other periods there exists a large body of received doctrine covering nearly the whole field of the moral relations of man and which no one thinks of questioning, backed as it is by the authority of all, or nearly all, persons supposed to possess knowledge enough to qualify them for giving an opinion on the subject. This state of things does not now exist in the civilised world. . . . The progress of enquiry has brought to light the insufficiency of the ancient doctrines but those who have made the investigation of social truths their occupation, have not yet sanctioned any new body of doctrine with their unanimous, or nearly unanimous, consent.[1]

In establishing the outlines of the history of Europe, Mill does not suggest that the Middle Ages were a period of social harmony and elevation of character: he is not, that is to say, a simple medieval romantic. He believes, nevertheless, that along with the great scientific and industrial advance of the three hundred years before he was born, a serious disturbance has occurred in the moral opinions and political structure of western Europe. The medieval feudal state and medieval feudal bond were characteristic of ages in which 'animal force' (seldom a good phrase in Mill) determined the nature of political relationships. To that extent the Middle Ages lacked qualities essential to a high stage of human development. But in some respects the Middle Ages had

[1] [J. S. Mill,] *The Spirit of the Age* (1831), [ed. Hayek, Chicago 1942, p. 32.]

4

something to recommend them. If the feudal bond depended on 'animal force', at least the feudal authority often performed a function. It was not just parasitical or materialistic; it provided protection to its dependents. So far as selfish interests deflected its agents from their duty, the feudal state, like any other, failed to conform to its principles, but, so far as it provided protection, it lived up to these principles. Similarly with the medieval Church. Mill saw in the medieval Church a serious defender not, as its members in their innocence may have supposed, of religion, but of cultivation and civilization in an age in which these things were more imperfectly admired than in some more recent periods. The Church was the means whereby medieval society provided itself with a body of common opinions. Social solidarity is a theme of which much will be heard in these pages: Mill's admiration for the medieval papacy (especially the Hildebrandine papacy) arose from his belief that the papacy in particular (and the medieval clergy in general) had performed with unusual adequacy what he took to be the main function of a clergy—provision of a generally received doctrine by which all actions could be judged, according to which all men could regulate their lives and to which they could expect their rulers to conform. This function can be performed whether the doctrine propagated is a true one or a false one: and it is clear that medieval solidarity was based on a doctrine— superstitious Christianity—to which Mill did not himself subscribe.

The Church, however, though it performed this function in the Middle Ages, had ceased to perform it by the beginning of the sixteenth century, and the Reformation is seen thereafter (at any rate on the continent) as the purely destructive dismantling of an institution which deserved to be dismantled because it had ceased to perform its historic function. The destruction of its spiritual authority, combined with the failure of Europe's monarchico-artistocratic régimes to perform the function *they* were supposed to perform, produced in reaction two important movements. It produced, in the first place, the eighteenth-century attempt to establish a rational science of society; and, secondly, what seems, in Mill's view, to have been partly a consequence of this and partly a consequence of the fact that 'the whole scheme of society and government in France had become a great Lie'—the French Revolution. Mill saw the French Revolution, not just as a great assertion of human liberty, but as the unfortunate consequence of the Enlightened attempt to articulate an abstract sociology. The abstract science of society was supported by, and resulted in, the foolish propositions of natural right theory. Natural right theory was foolish because it ignored the need to marry abstract doctrines to particular circumstances; it produced disastrous consequences in France when attempts were made to put its conclusions into practice without reference to the circumstances in which it was applied. Mill had no doubt that the monarchy and aristocracy deserved what they got in the revolutionary upheaval: but he did not for that reason admire, or excuse, the destruction that went with it. One of the few aspects of French history between 1750 and 1850 which pleased Mill was the removal of Christianity from the dominant position it had held for so long. Catholic Christianity had, he implies, quoting Comte, already in the seventeenth-century 'stopt short while the world had gone on [and] become a hindrance to progress instead of a promoter of it'. Fénélon and St Vincent de Paul, Bossuet and de Maistre were great men: but the French Church and its leaders insisted on maintaining positions unsuitable to the age in which they lived. The progress

6

of opinion, the social inadequacy of the ruling class and the failure of the Church to perform the tasks it performed in the Middle Ages had had their effect: by 1830, Mill thought, no damage could be done to French social solidarity (or the acceptability of enlightened opinions) by attacking Christianity, since Christianity had (as it had not in England) once and for all been decisively dethroned.

In England conditions were different, for a variety of reasons. There, as in France, the Reformation had destroyed the dominance of the Roman Church only when that church had forfeited the respect it originally deserved to claim. But in England Protestantism took deeper root, not only ecclesiastically and politically, but in increasing the intelligence and practical involvement of the great body of the population. Protestantism, unlike Catholicism, succeeded 'in cultivating the intelligence and conscience of the individual believer'. Protestant rejection of the tendency to assume that belief was to be accepted from a priest 'meant that there was the strongest inducement to every believer, however humble, to seek culture and to profit by it'. Because of the character of the Church of England, English Protestants did not profit as much from education as Scottish and New England Protestants did. Amongst both these groups 'an amount of education was carried down to the poorest of the people . . . [as] every peasant expounded the Bible to his family . . . [and] brought down to the humblest layman . . . [a] sharpening and strengthening exercise, . . . [a] discipline in abstraction and reasoning' which enabled 'Scotland . . . [to supply] the greater part of Europe with professors for its universities and educated and skilled workmen for its practical arts'.[1] England was not so fortunate, but even in England, Protestantism

---

[1] [Mill, *Auguste*] *Comte and Positivism* [Michigan 1961 and London 1866], pp. 112–13.

made a popular mark which Catholicism could never have made—with the result that, at the beginning of the nineteenth century, Christianity, far from being dead, was so integral a part of the dominant orthodoxy, that anyone who attacked it openly would merely damage the causes he wished to advance.

If Christianity was not dead, however, the Established Church was, or, to judge by its performance, should be deemed to be. And not the Established Church only, but the State also. Mill sees English history after 1660 as a record of the subjection to sinister, self-interested nest-feathering of the authority and power of Church and State. 'Practical Toryism' was dominant, not, it may be noted, practical 'Whiggery'; and 'practical Tory-ism' was not the stimulating 'speculative Toryism' of Southey and Coleridge but 'simply . . . being *in* and availing yourself of your comfortable position *inside* the vehicle without minding the poor devils who are freezing *outside*'.[1] The successors of the medieval clergy who had defended 'the arts' against 'animal force' could now not defend their own dogmas against enlightened assault. The combined effect of a theology which, in Paley's hands, made fear of doing otherwise the reason for doing right, and of a clergy which neither used its endowment to maintain general cultivation nor numbered the most cultivated intellects amongst its members, had been con-siderable. The English State and English Church were not, in this caricature of the history of the two cen-turies following the Restoration, institutions to attract loyalty or supply a generally agreed doctrinal basis for social and political action. The alliance between Church and State, or landowner and clergy, though guaranteeing ecclesiastical endowment in return for

---

[1] J. S. Mill to John Sterling, October 20–22, 1831; ed. H. S. R. Elliot, *The Letters of John Stuart Mill*, London 1910, vol. i, p. 14.

clerical political acquiescence, guaranteed performance neither of the religious nor of the secular functions of the State. The universities had become idle theological seminaries without learning or intellect: landowning was carried on too much for profit, and with too little conception of social use. The State was dominated by the territorial aristocracy; the sinister interest of clergy in their endowments, and landowners in their profits, ensured that the alliance, which in the Middle Ages had sometimes been fruitful, had so seriously degenerated since 1660 that the politically dominant classes seemed to have come near to renouncing altogether the attempt to perform their proper social function.

Nor had the Industrial Revolution and the development of democratic doctrine produced any marked, or permanent, improvement. The period of invention and industrial growth had made it possible to maintain a greatly increased population; it provided an excellent example of human intelligence improving Nature. The democratic revolution in political thinking had established one important truth—that rulers owed duties, not just to their own judgement of the social interest, but to the people's judgement of the interest of society as a whole. Democratic assumptions made it possible to conceive that everyone should play some part in government, that no one would want indefinitely to accept the authority of his social superiors. These were serious, permanent gains, Mill seems to have thought: he made no attempt to question them. Whatever their merits, however, these two revolutions had dominated English life since 1750 and brought with them consequences which Mill did not admire. Industrial expansion had created a class of practically energetic entrepreneurs. It had produced also acquisitive entrepreneurs who supposed that accumulation of wealth was the sole object of human existence, who did not understand that the 'struggle for riches' is a 'coarse' phase in human history likely to be satisfying only to 'coarse minds', and who would, therefore, have to be educated if they were to fulfil their social responsibilities. Without education of the intellect, these responsibilities would not be fulfilled: if they were not, manufacturers would fail to play their part in building a society in which 'addition to just institutions, the increase of mankind shall be under the deliberate guidance of judicious foresight, [and where] the conquests made from the powers of nature by the intellect and energy of scientific discoverers become the common property of the species, and the means of improving and elevating the universal lot'.[1] If the Industrial Revolution had made possible a vast increase in population, part of this increase had occurred amongst an uncultivated proletariat, which was tending by its physical presence to endanger that mental solitude on which worth-while cultivation depends. Mill did not deny that the industrial proletariat could benefit from education, or that it might, once offered the opportunity, be willing to be educated. In existing conditions, however, the process would be a long one; the increase in population, combined with the spread of democratic doctrine, had produced a society whose political and ecclesiastical leaders had abandoned the attempt to supply a range of universally accepted teaching; in these circumstances it was likely that vulgarity and philistinism would triumph.

It is important to be clear about the character of Mill's suspicion of the increase in the numbers, and power, of the democratic element. He feared that democracy would destroy the higher cultivation; he thought it would do so because of its 'collective mediocrity'. But

---

[1] [J. S. Mill], *Principles* [*of Political Economy* (1848), ed. Sir W. J. Ashley, London 1920], pp. 749–751.

the collective mediocrity he fears is not just the collective mediocrity of manual labourers whose willingness to be educated (given the chance) he rates high. What he fears is 'collective mediocrity' wherever it is to be found —the mediocrity of landowning philistines who mis-govern and the mediocrity of plutocratic philistines who have such limited conceptions of the range of human possibility: the mediocrity of the vast body of citizens whose intellectual and moral development has been arrested at the stage of sensual enjoyment, and the mediocrity of a clergy whose eyes do not rise above interested enjoyment of the fruits of offices. This mediocrity is to be feared and fought, partly because it is bad in itself, partly because its refusal to be self-conscious about principle hampers the restoration of that medieval condition in which at least men had the opportunity to know what their principles were, because the clergy took the trouble to tell them.

Habit, when based on good principles, is not, in Mill's eyes, an intolerably fallible guide to action: but habit, when based on 'the despotism of custom', or refusal to be self-conscious about principle, is. The philistinism for which he reserves his sharpest criticism is the philistinism which, because it declines to discuss, or is incapable of discussing, the practical implication of moral principle, allows conduct to be dominated by 'sinister interests'. This is likely to occur whenever men lose hold of the theoretical grounds on which their conduct should be founded. It has occurred, Mill asserts, in England and Europe to an increasing extent in the last three hundred years. The age is a mediocre age, in Mill's view, because old opinions are dead, and because of a reluctance to probe the superficial authority of habit in order to see what body of principles validated habitual commitments in the first place. The process of moral and political questioning is essential to social health: if it is not undertaken, Europe will stand in danger of becoming, as at one stage Mill thought the United States *had* become—another China, in which the crust of old habit concealed, at the root of the human condition, not active intelligence energetically improving nature, but sloth, torpor and the intolerance of mental and moral indifference.

The situation Mill feels called on to deal with—the historic mission it is his business to fulfil—is to provide a body of commanding doctrine which, by stimulating the higher intelligence of all citizens, will produce, as a consequence, not individualistic anarchy, but that sense of active participation which well-regulated societies alone are capable of providing. Mill is attempting to establish a binding philosophy, a moral, ethical and social doctrine which will both tell men what their duties are, and induce that sense of common participation, of which the great changes in European society, and the decay of old opinions, have deprived them. This is Mill's central concern: the central portion of the explanatory section of this book explains the content, and philosophical basis, of that 'moral and intellectual ascendancy [which], once exercised by priests, must in time pass into the hands of philosophers, and [which] will naturally do so when they become sufficiently unanimous, and in other respects worthy to possess it'.[1]

Before reaching this point, however, it is necessary to ask why Mill supposed that Christianity could no longer supply this body of received opinion. It is necessary to ask this because there are suggestions (particularly in *The Utility of Religion*) that Mill does not mind *which* doctrine is generally accepted—so long as *a* doctrine succeeds in supplying a basis for social action. Nor does he deny

[1] [J. S. Mill,] *Autobiography* [(1873), London 1873, p. 212.]

the 'moral grandeur' of Christ, the great merit of his contribution to the improvement of mankind or the profound effect Christianity has had on the history of the world. The moral teachings of Christianity are a worthy part of the human endeavour to establish a binding morality, and will not, Mill thinks, readily be lost. Though part of the permanent morality of mankind, however, they are not the whole of it. Christian morality is objectionable to Mill (so far as it *is* objectionable) because, in spite of the moral grandeur of its founder, it teaches not a comprehensive morality, but a partial one. The theology which has been overlaid across Christ's teaching fails to deal with all sorts of situation; it neglects for example (as the Koran does not) to concern itself with the duties of rulers.

Its ideal is negative rather than positive; passive rather than active; Innocence rather than Nobleness; Abstinence from Evil, rather than energetic Pursuit of Good; [and in] . . . hold[ing] out the hope of heaven and the threat of hell, as the appointed and appropriate motives to a virtuous life; . . . [does what it can] to give to human morality an essentially selfish character, by disconnecting each man's feelings of duty from the interests of his fellow creatures, except so far as a self-interested inducement is offered to him for consulting them.[1]

The medieval Church performed a valuable service both in the Middle Ages and in the march of history: but the intolerance of Christians, their reluctance to admit that truth may be known by non-Christians, and the tendency to mistake *their* part of truth for the whole, mean that, in an age where comprehensiveness of approach is essential, it is necessary to supersede the partial Christian truths by a more comprehensive account of the character of human existence.

Comte had argued (and Mill accepts the position)

[1] [J. S. Mill,] *On Liberty* [(1859), ed. R. B. McCallum, Oxford 1946, pp. 43–4.]

that the history of each society passes through three phases—a theological phase, in which every action is attributed to direct divine intervention, a metaphysical phase, in which everything is attributed to general laws, and a positive or scientific phase in which explanation is given by reference to the specific laws of the particular subject that is under consideration. A great deal of questionable thinking goes on at the point at which Mill attempts to establish the scientific character of his moral and political doctrines: but, at a fundamental level, he relegates Christianity to, at best, a place in the metaphysical stage, and dismisses the cosmology and morality on which it depends as unsuitable to the scientific, comprehensive period for which he supposed himself to be writing. Intellectual progress had made it difficult to accept the truths of Christianity: for 'its divine message, assuming it to be such, has been authenticated by credentials so insufficient, that they fail to convince a large proportion of the strongest and most cultivated minds, and the tendency to disbelieve them appears to grow with the growth of scientific knowledge and critical discrimination'. More will be said about this in a moment: but it is important to understand that Mill supposed his task—of finding a body of commanding doctrine—a worth-while one because, in the scientific, cosmopolitan age on which mankind was embarking, the particularity, intolerance, arrogance and temporal irrelevance of Christianity would prevent it matching up to the oecumenical problems which that phase of history would present.

However, if Christianity was to be superseded (because the failure of Christians had made supersession necessary), one at least of its features was to remain. If the clergy had failed to hold the attention of the nation's highest intellect, that is not to say that *any* clergy would be similarly inadequate. The intellectual bankruptcy of the Church of England did not mean that the function which the Anglican clergy *ought* to be performing could not be performed by another, more comprehensive, body of superior minds. The medieval clergy had provided a corporate defence of the cultivation that was appropriate to the age in which they lived; there ought, in a healthy society, to be successors who would perform the same function in a manner, and with doctrines, suitable to a later age. The established clergy could no longer do so (because of its intellectual decrepitude): but why could not superior intellect itself perform the function? The truths of Christianity were partial truths: the clergy had in any case lost sight of their obligation to them. What was necessary now was to endow, and support, a class which would fertilize men's understanding of truth and propagate knowledge of it, so as to ensure that the homogeneity of opinion which the medieval Spiritual Power had done its best to supply would restore that moral self-confidence on which healthy societies are founded. The body to be commissioned to undertake this task is the clerisy: since it is of central importance in Mill's social and political philosophy, we must ask what its functions are intended to be.

In what way, if at all, Mill's clerisy is to be distinguished from a clergy is a question to which the answer will be delayed until an account has been given of the doctrine it is supposed to teach. Nor will an answer be given yet to the question: is it a religion that the clerisy is supposed to propagate? For the moment it is sufficient to say that, whatever Mill thinks about the relationship between utility and religion, he has no doubt about the importance of education in inducing men to feel consciousness of responsible membership of the community in which they live. Supernatural sanctions may be helpful or they may not: but 'the power of education', in the widest sense, 'is almost boundless'[1]: and the function of the clerisy is to provide that body of explanatory fact and received doctrine on the existence of which all formal education, and all the influences of formal education, always rest.

The clerisy, he says, quoting Coleridge

'in its primary acceptation and original intention comprehended the learned of all denominations, the sages and professors of the law and jurisprudence, of medicine and physiology, of music, of military and civil architecture, with the mathematical as the common organ of the preceeding; in short, all the so-called liberal arts and sciences, the possession and application of which constitute the civilisation of a country, as well as the theological'. The 'theological learned' were essential to the scheme because 'under the name of theology or divinity were contained the interpretation of languages, the conservation and tradition of past events . . . and the ground knowledge, the *prima scientia*, as it was named—philosophy, or the doctrine and discipline of ideas . . . because [in other words] the science of theology was the root and the trunk of the knowledge of civilised man'.

Their position in this respect was not achieved because the members of the 'theological order . . . were priests whose office was to conciliate the invisible powers, and to superintend the interests that survive the grave': indeed, their sacerdotal (and even Christian) character, was, in relation to the national Church, 'a blessed accident, a providential boon, a grace of God'. The business of the national Church, or nationalty of the nation, and the only end to which its endowments should be put, is to be an instrument of civilization, and the conclusion to which Mill presses Coleridge's argument is that this is 'a theory under which the Royal Society might claim a part of the Church property with as good right as the bench of bishops'.

The State . . . [he adds] having decided that the Church of England does not fulfill the object for which the nationalty

<hr>

[1] [J. S. Mill,] *Three Essays on Religion* [(1874), London 1874, p. 82.]

16

was intended, might transfer its endowments to any other ecclesiastical body, or to any other body not ecclesiastical, which it deemed more competent to fulfill those objects; might establish any other sect, or all sects, or no sect at all, if it should deem that in the divided condition of religious opinion in this country, the State can no longer with advantage attempt the complete religious instruction of its people, but must for the present content itself with providing secular instruction, and such religious teaching, if any, as all can take part in; leaving each sect to apply to its own communion that which they all agree in considering as the keystone of the arch.

The nationalty, or national property (which is Coleridge's way of describing the endowments held by the Church of England) is therefore

destined for 'the support and maintenance of a permanent class or order, with the following duties. A certain smaller number were to remain at the fountainheads of the humanities, in cultivating and enlarging the knowledge already possessed, and in watching over the interests of physical and moral science; being likewise the instructors of such as constituted, or were to constitute, the remaining more numerous classes of the order. The members of this latter and far more numerous body were to be distributed throughout the country, so as not to leave even the smallest integral part or division without a resident guide, guardian, and instructor; the objects and final intention of the whole order being these—to preserve the stores and to guard the treasures of past civilization, and thus to bind the present with the past; to perfect and add to the same, and thus to connect the present with the future; but especially to diffuse through the whole community, and to every native entitled to its laws and rights, that quantity and quality of knowledge which was indispensable both for the understanding of those rights, and for the performance of the duties correspondent; finally, to secure for the nation, if not a superiority over the neighbouring states, yet an equality at least, in that character of general civilization, which equally with, or rather more than, fleets, armies and revenue, forms the ground of its defensive and offensive power'.[1]

[1] [J. S. Mill,] *Coleridge* [(1840), ed. F. R. Leavis, *Mill on Coleridge and Bentham*, London 1950, pp. 142–6.]

17

That is what the clerisy is: its business is to provide a body of received opinions. How is to be maintained? How will it exert authority? What will be the extent of its power?

About these questions Mill is on some occasions specific and on others vague, but, if his opinions about the clerisy are tied together, one finds in his work something resembling a blue-print for its sustenance. It is not merely that criticism is directed in *Principles of Political Economy* against the assumption of 'older economists' that society ought always to be expanding in numbers and scale. It is that one aspect of Mill's preference for the stationary State—the State in which expansion is checked by deliberate restriction of population growth—is that it will both increase the access to solitude open to the higher minds, and maximize the amount of cultivation open to the rest of mankind.

It is not good for man to be kept perforce at all times in the presence of his species. A world from which solitude is extirpated is a very poor ideal. Solitude, in the sense of being often alone, is essential to any depth of meditation or of character; and solitude in the presence of natural beauty and grandeur, is the cradle of thoughts and aspirations which are not only good for the individual, but which society could ill do without. Nor is there much satisfaction in contemplating the world with nothing left to the spontaneous activity of nature; with every rood of land brought into cultivation, which is capable of growing food for human beings; every flowery waste or natural pasture ploughed up, all quadrupeds or birds which are not domesticated for man's use exterminated as his rivals for food, every hedgerow or superfluous tree rooted out, and scarcely a place left where a wild shrub or flower could grow without being eradicated as a weed in the name of improved agriculture. If the earth [Mill concludes] must lose that great portion of its pleasantness which it owes to things that the unlimited increase of wealth and population would extirpate from it, for the mere purpose of enabling it to support a larger, but not a better or a happier population, I sincerely hope, for the sake of posterity, that they will be content to be stationary, long before necessity compels them to it.[1]

In a stationary state, furthermore, where expansion is not the overriding motive of social policy, it will be easier to break down inequalities of wealth, to destroy the greater inherited disparities and ensure that the middle rank of society—the rank of educated people— will have that 'moderate' financial 'independence' on which mental cultivation sometimes depends, whilst being neither too far distant, nor too greatly alienated, from an improved proletariat. In these circumstances

society would exhibit these leading features; a well-paid and affluent body of labourers; no enormous fortunes, except what were earned and accumulated during a single lifetime; but a much larger body of persons than at present, not only exempt from the coarser toils, but with sufficient leisure, both physical and mental, from mechanical details, to cultivate freely the graces of life, and afford examples of them to the classes less favourably circumstanced for their growth.[2]

Mill nowhere actually says so, but it is difficult to avoid feeling that the distrust he feels of the greater inherited inequalities arises from the assumption—a curious one in view of the history of the seventeenth and eighteenth centuries—that territorial magnates, and other owners of an undue amount of inherited wealth, were less likely to be interested in mental cultivation than others might be, and that his moderate economic egalitarianism followed from the consistently held belief that more equal distribution of wealth would make it easier to replace existing styles of mental cultivation by his own more moralistic sort.

The cultivated classes cannot be maintained, how- ever, merely by provision of financial independence;

[1] *Principles*, pp. 750-1.   [2] *Principles*, p. 750.

educational institutions have to be provided. One chief function of the medieval Church had been to maintain general cultivation: Mill saw no reason why the 'theological seminaries' on which the post-Reformation Church of England had depended, should not be turned into agents of general cultivation also. Oxford and Cambridge had, in his view, long ceased to contribute to research: nor did they fertilize the tradition of general cultivation on which 'intellectual *power* . . . and the intensest *love of truth*' depended. They had, on the contrary, become sectarian seminaries, though this was not their original function. Their endowments had been given in the first place as much for cultivation as for religion, and should now be converted into the high point and pivot of a system of national education. The object would be to ensure propagation of the highest learning and best opinions throughout the nation,

and the very first step towards [university] reform should be to unsectarianise [universities] wholly—not by the paltry measure of allowing Dissenters to come and be taught orthodox sectarianism, but by putting an end to sectarian teaching altogether. The principle itself of dogmatic religion, dogmatic morality, dogmatic philosophy, is what requires to be rooted out; not any particular manifestation of that principle.[1]

The essay on *The Right and Wrong of State Interference with Corporation and Church Property* argues vigorously, and casuistically, against the view that the specific terms of a founder's will should be binding in perpetuity, and offers a sustained plea for diverting university and church endowments from their existing 'sectarian' purpose to this general educational one, with a view, as he says in describing the original purpose of church endowments,

[1] J. S. Mill, 'Civilization' (1836) in *Dissertations and Discussions*, London 1859, vol. 1, pp. 200–1.

to 'the spiritual culture of the people of England'.[1] The sort of education he wants is not, in modern terms, what would be called 'research' (though dons should contribute more extensively to research than existing dons did): nor should it be vocational or professional. University education, on the contrary, in Mill's view, is the process of infusing that general culture which enables professional and vocational activities to yield to the general principles by which they should be guided.[2]

Mill was not, in political matters, an optimist; he had no illusion about the difficulty the clerisy would find in making its influence felt. Philistinism at all levels would operate against it. Existing political arrangements were unpromising. It was intolerable that 'at present, by universal admission, it is becoming more and more difficult for anyone who has only talents and character to gain admission into the House of Commons'. There were 'hundreds of able men of independent thought who ... have by their writings, or their exertions in some field of public usefulness, made themselves ... approved by a few persons in almost every district of the kingdom', and it was inconvenient, in relation to the contribution these men could make, that 'the only persons who can get elected are those who possess local influence, or make their way by lavish expenditure, or who, on the invitation of three or four tradesmen or attorneys, are sent down by one of the two great parties from their London clubs, as men whose votes the party can depend on under all circumstances'.[3] 'The very *élite* of the country'[4]

[1] J. S. Mill, 'The Right and Wrong of State Interference with Corporation and Church Property' (1833) in *Dissertations and Discussions*, London 1859, vol. 1, p. 12 and *passim*.
[2] Cf. [J. S. Mill,] *Inaugural Address* [delivered to the *University of St. Andrews* (1867), 1867, pp. 5-7.]
[3] [J. S. Mill, *Considerations on*] *Representative Government* [(1861), ed. R. B. McCallum, Oxford, 1946, p. 197.]
[4] *Op. cit.*, p. 198.

ought to be represented in Parliament: they should be spared the uncertainties of constituency politics, and, for this reason, if for no other, proposals for national Electoral rolls for the election of candidates of national reputation (Hare's scheme) should be adopted.[1] Mill did not suppose that cultivated persons would be likely, in the near future, to set the tone of the House of Commons: but he hoped that

if the presence in the representative assembly can be insured of even a few of the first minds in the country, though the remainder consist only of average minds, the influence of these leading spirits is sure to make itself sensibly felt in the general deliberations, even though they be known to be, in many respects, opposed to the tone of popular opinion and feeling.[2]

These 'first minds' (which he elsewhere calls 'instructed minds', and by which he seems to mean persons of literary and professional, rather than political, distinction) would compel 'the representatives of the majority ... when any differences arose ... to meet the arguments of the instructed few by reasons, at least apparently, as cogent': 'the champions of unpopular doctrines would not put forth their arguments merely in books and periodicals read only by their own side; the opposing ranks would meet face to face and hand to hand ... there would be a fair comparison of their intellectual strength in the presence of the country'[3]; and a tendency would emerge to raise discussion of principle to a level higher than it had reached in the aristocratic House of his time. Mill at no period in his life expected the clerisy to make a ready impact on political life: he is consistent, at one level, in not wanting it to dominate. Comte's plan for government by alliance between the largest owners of industrial wealth—the feudal magnates of the industrial age—and a Spiritual Power of scientific

[1] *Op. cit.*, p. 197.   [2] *Op. cit.*, p. 200.   [3] *Op. cit.*, p. 199.

scholars sustaining their influence by centralized education and a controlled press, showed what a great mind could do when it lost respect for individuality. Nevertheless, at another level, Mill hoped the clerisy would succeed, without coercion or compulsion, in making the same sort of impact on society as Comte's Spiritual Power was designed to make *with* them. The struggle, he knew, would be a long one; the people might be willing to learn, but willingness to learn was not the same as capacity for learning. Unless education were compulsory (though provided as much as possible by private agency), the impact would not be great. Unless the clerisy were strongly entrenched and strongly supported, its teachings would not make their mark on society as a whole: strength of support and strength of entrenchment would not come until the desire for education was matched by its availability. There are many facets to the assertion that Mill treats positive education and general cultivation as a kind of religion. Others will be dealt with later. What matters here is that, whereas the dominance of Comte's Spiritual Power was to be maintained by governmental coercion, Mill's spiritual power, and its spiritual teaching, was to grow by persuasion in the minds of the people. Mill, no less than Comte, looked forward to a period when there would, once more, be a spiritual consensus: but he wished the consensus to grow by *rational* persuasion and *rational* argument based on *rational* education, not by suppression, violence and force. It was obviously impossible forcibly to impose 'positive' opinions on the English aristocracy. The English aristocracy was heavily entrenched and had no intention of renouncing political power. Similarly with the constantly increasing class of manual labourers. They, too, could not be *directed* to believe one thing or another. Paternalism, if it ever existed, was no longer feasible: the tutelary relationship

23

on which feudalism had rested could in present conditions no longer be justified. 'All privileged and powerful classes . . . [had] used their power in the interest of their own selfishness, and . . . indulged their self-importance in despising, and not in lovingly caring for, those who were, in their estimation, degraded, by being under the necessity of working for their benefit'.[1] It ceased, moreover, to be possible to treat the class of manual labourers as being in need of care and protection once 'they were taught to read, and allowed access to newspapers and political tracts . . . dissenting preachers . . . [factories] . . . railways . . . and the franchise'.[2] 'Mere authority and *prestige* of superiors' would no longer be sufficient to command their allegiance :[3] they would make up their own minds what sort of authority to follow, though that is not to say that they would not, so long as they *are* left free to judge with the resources of educated minds, 'feel respect for superiority of intellect and knowledge, and defer much to the opinions, on any subject, of those whom they think well acquainted with it'.[4] 'The prospect of the future', Mill concludes, 'depends on the degree in which they can be made rational beings',[5] and he might, with suitable emendations, have applied to the impact of education on the proletariat what he wrote of the impact of critical self-examination on the aristocracy.

Let no-one think it is nothing [he wrote in the essay on *Coleridge*] to accustom people to give a reason for their opinion, be the opinion ever so untenable, the reason ever so insufficient. A person accustomed to submit his fundamental tenets to the test of reason will be more open to the dictates of reason, on every other point . . . 'Lord, enlighten thou our enemies' should be the prayer of every true Reformer; sharpen their wits, give acuteness to their perceptions, and consecutiveness and clearness to their reasoning powers. . . .

---

[1] *Principles*, p. 754. [2] *Op. cit.*, p. 756. [3] *Op. cit.*, p. 758.
[4] *Op. cit.*, p. 759. [5] *Op. cit.*, p. 757.

For ourselves, we are not so blinded by our particular opinions as to be ignorant that in this and in every other country of Europe, the great mass of the owners of large property, and of all the classes intimately connected with the owners of large property, are, and must be expected to be, in the main, Conservative. To suppose that so mighty a body can be without immense influence in the commonwealth, or to lay plans for effecting great changes, either spiritual or temporal, in which they are left out of the question, would be the height of absurdity. Let those who desire such changes, ask themselves if they are content that these classes should be, and remain, to a man, banded against them; and what progress they expect to make, or by what means, unless a process of preparation shall be going on in the minds of these very classes; not by the impracticable method of converting them from Conservatives into Liberals, but by their being led to adopt one liberal opinion after another, as a part of Conservatism itself. The first step to this is to inspire them with the desire to systematize and rationalize their own actual creed: and the feeblest attempt to do this has an intrinsic value; far more, then, one which has so much in it, both of moral goodness and true insight, as the philosophy of Coleridge.[1]

The function of the clerisy, of the pursuit of the higher cultivation, of universal education, of the separate electoral roll, of commitment to the stationary State and greater general equality, and of the diversion of church funds to secular purposes is, then, to develop, in the moral and intellectual decay characteristic of an age of unfixed opinions, a body of commanding doctrine which will enable citizens to have a positive basis for their conceptions of political duty, and to restore that sense of solidarity which comes from general rational agreement about the method of determining the character of the good society. Whatever the means Mill advocates in order to achieve solidarity and rational participation, there can be no doubt, and there is no ambiguity about the fact, that he believes this to be a proper function of

[1] *Coleridge*, pp. 167–8.

human society: and that there is, beyond the libertarian character of the means, an assumption of the fundamental homogeneity of all rational judgement. This is an important assumption, and it is necessary now to ask—what is the character of this social solidarity? What sort of homogeneity is assumed? and what is the content of the means Mill thinks useful in attempting to establish it?

CHAPTER 2

THE DOCTRINE

Mill claimed, it is platitudinous to say, to be a utilitarian: so far as he located the desirability of actions in their consequences, he most certainly was a utilitarian. It is difficult, however, to reconcile his use of the principle of utility with the use to which Bentham and James Mill had put it; any attempt to understand it on this basis is unlikely to penetrate its nebulous comprehensiveness. The principle of utility is used by Mill, not as his predecessors used it, but as a sort of pious slogan with which to convince himself that he was not departing too radically from the tradition in which he had grown up. No criticism need be made of Mill because he inserts into *utility all* the good ends to which human endeavour has aspired: but its meaning, nevertheless, and the part it plays in his doctrine, can best be understood, not by approaching it in a narrow political spirit, but by asking, in the first place—what sort of life and what sort of conduct is it to which the aspirations of mankind should be directed? For, once the question is put in this form, the answer will be seen to entail, not a circumscribed account of *governmental* and *political* obligation, but a set of universally binding guides to individual and social action, a body of beliefs that relieve men, and society, from the disorders, imperfections and vulgarities which come from conformity to credulous, unelevated, unreflective *habit*. Whatever may be thought of attempts to show that Bentham was proposing a comprehensive objectively-binding ethic, there can be no doubt that Mill himself attempted what Bentham may not in fact have done. Mill, even when he least realizes he is doing this, is doing it: any account which considers his utilitarianism in a manner less extensive is unlikely to do justice to its character.

At the centre of Mill's ethical teaching are to be found, involved with the principle of utility, a set of doctrines about liberty, a set of doctrines about education and a set of doctrines about the desirability of recurrent critical self-examination. None of these doctrines can be understood without reference to the others. All tend in the same direction: the content of each is the same as the content of the others. The conception he has in mind, the position to which he wishes to persuade, is the desirability of creating a society which is morally homogeneous and intellectually healthy, because most men (including the poor) not only have the opportunity to reach, but succeed in reaching, an educational level sufficient to enable them to reflect on the content of their ethical and social purposes, to replace customary deference to arbitrarily established authority by rational deference to elevated intellect, and to reach (in virtue of rational reflection) agreed, superior judgements about the character of the means by which to decide what actions are right. This is deliberate commitment to persuade to a self-conscious ethic—an outcome of the belief that only ethical or political positions which have been arrived at as a result of articulate reflection and disinterested motivation have binding authority. Mill has sufficient respect for custom to recognize that a great deal of human action must always be taken without immediate reflective questioning: he accepts the fact that, once good principles have been established as a basis for conduct, they will not need to be subjected to critical examination on every occasion. Nevertheless, above the level at which habit can judge the rationality of

28

social convention, is a body of what Mill calls *principles* to which commitment must be given self-consciously, deliberately and after critical consideration. Each age has a principle, or set of principles, which is more fundamental than the rest: the integrity of an age (or society) is measured by the extent to which the principle is grasped, and assented to, by those who are part of it. So far as a man, or group, investigates the rationality, or truth, of a principle of action, he is acting reasonably: so far as he accepts it on trust, out of blind habit or in obedience to custom, he fails in an essential form of activity. Mill's view of history is dominated by consciousness of conflict between, on the one hand, prejudice and habit, and, on the other, the higher reasoning of the reflective mind, which succeeds, as a rational creation, in determining its motives for itself. All human history testifies to the existence of the struggle; the destiny of superior intellect in contemporary society is to carry its victories to a higher stage of accomplishment.

Mill's position, however, is not just the simple assertion of a crude, vulgar, intellectualized libertarianism. He is saying that all men have an obligation, and, once they have been educated, have the opportunity, to submit their own, and society's actions, to rational questioning. They can, in other words, and ought to, ask always for the reason for an action, or the principle an institution is supposed to embody; if the action has no reason and the institution seems to be in conflict with principle, they should abandon the one and make the other conform more closely. All men have an obligation to do this. Opinions need not be accepted because they have *been* accepted ('received' is his word) in the past: nor need they be accepted because the majority have come to accept them in the present. The individual judgement is

29

free: a man's destiny is to exercise this aspect of his rational freedom. Truth may well be found in the judgement of an individual: an eccentric individual, defying the collective judgement of society (which may also be its collective mediocrity) may well be justified by this possibility.

Nevertheless, if it is the individual's duty (and particularly the educated individual's duty) to submit all action to scrutiny by self-conscious ethical judgement, Mill is not advocating anarchic assertion of individual freedom. The emphasis, in Mill's justification of freedom, is neither on its intrinsic goodness nor on any belief man may have in its natural rightness, but on the fact that a free individual is more likely than an unfree one to contribute to the higher cultivation. This is why he advocates recurring critical self-examination. He does not commit himself to it because it is naturally good or because it is 'natural' to man to want it. Nature is not, in Mill's view, good: all the good in the world is the result of human effort to improve Nature. If Mill comes near to regarding reflective questioning as good in itself, without regard to its consequences, he makes clear his belief that a questioning which did not produce general agreement about the desirability of the higher cultivation would have failed to be a desirable questioning. Mill can face the possibility of initial disagreement between the judgements of reflecting men because he assumes that minds which have been properly educated will ultimately agree in their view of the grounds on which individual freedom should be limited. His desire to provide universally acceptable opinions for his age and society has been mentioned already: but it should be mentioned in this connection again. What Mill hoped for from the process of critical questioning, what he assumed to be the natural outcome of the probing for reasons, is the establishment in a healthy society (almost, indeed, as proof of the existence of a healthy society) of a body of definitive opinions whose authority is no longer in doubt because they have been reached by agreed, rational, self-evident reasoning. Mill accused Comte of being 'a morality-intoxicated man'.[1] By this he meant that Comte, seeing that 'egoism is bound, and should be taught, always to give way to the well-understood interests of enlarged altruism'[2] drew the erroneous conclusion that 'because the good of the human race is the ultimate standard of right and wrong . . . [therefore] the good of others is the only inducement on which we should allow ourselves to act'.[3] Mill does not, at the superficial level, make this mistake. He is articulately hostile to 'unity' and 'systematisation', particularly when they are, in Comte's scheme, connected with the spiritual despotism of the learned. 'Why' he asks 'this universal systematising, systematising, systematising? Why is it necessary that all human life should point but to one object, and be cultivated into a system of means to a single end?':[4] and one thinks, at this point, that Mill is as libertarian as he wishes to appear.

Yet, if one looks more closely, his reasons and expectations are scarcely less 'unified' than Comte's. He says, it is true, that 'mankind who, after all are made up of single human beings, obtain a greater sum of happiness when each pursues his own . . . than when each makes the good of the rest his only object'.[5] Individual 'happiness' in Mill, however, means not any happiness the individual happens to desire, but the sort of elevated happiness men should (because they do?) desire. 'Mankind' would not, in Mill's view, 'obtain a greater sum of

---

[1] *Comte and Positivism*, pp. 139–40.   [2] *Op. cit.*, p. 139.
[3] *Op. cit.*, p. 138.   [4] *Op. cit.*, p. 141.
[5] *Op. cit.*, pp. 141–2.

happiness' if each individual pursued an uninstructed idea of 'happiness'. When Mill uses *happiness*, he means the happiness that *rational* reflection would approve, not *any* pleasure a man *happens* to pursue. This greatly limits the range of acceptable action. When connected with the provision that happiness must be pursued 'under the rules and conditions required by the good of the rest',[1] that 'it is incumbent on everyone to restrain the pursuit of his personal objects within the limits consistent with the essential interests of others'[2] and that 'it is the province of ethical science to determine . . . what those limits are',[3] it compels us to conclude that, although his ethical injunctions are not the same as Comte's, they are, in spite of the disingenuousness of the language in which they are surrounded, quite as effective in proscribing large ranges of conduct. This is not surprising: everyone who sets up as an ethical teacher condemns or excludes other sorts of ethical teaching. Mill is at liberty to criticize Comte for 'prodigiously exaggerat[ing] . . . moral restraints', and Calvinism for failing to perceive that 'between the region of duty and that of sin there is an intermediate space, the region of positive worthiness'.[4] It is reasonable to claim, if as a utilitarian he wants to, that 'spontaneity' must be maintained if we are to approve the efforts men make to increase the good of others beyond the 'standard of altruism' which *all* have an *obligation* to reach.[5] He is free to assert that 'sufficient gratification of the [egoistic propensities], short of excess, but up to the measure which renders the enjoyment greatest, is almost always favourable to the benevolent affections' and he may well be right to suggest that 'demanding no more . . . as a rule of conduct . . . [than that] no more should be attempted than to prevent

[1] *Op. cit.*, p. 141.   [2] *Op. cit.*, p. 143.   [3] *Ibid.*
[4] *Op. cit.*, p. 142.   [5] *Op. cit.*, p. 143.

people from doing harm to others, or omitting to do such good as they have undertaken . . . society, in any tolerable circumstances, obtains much more'.[1]

All these things it may be legitimate to say; what is not legitimate is, in the same breath, to suppose that these injunctions are the necessary conclusions of ethical philosophy, binding on all society, or that they leave room for the belief that 'there could be more than one road to human happiness'.[2] By the side of Comte's, Mill's happiness has 'more', as he says 'than one ingredient in it': but he is saying, nevertheless, that there is *a* doctrine, one doctrine, defining the nature of happiness and the means to achieve it, and that that doctrine is binding. 'The means' involve proper disposition of the motives through critical self-examination, and sensitivity to the highest rationality humanity can reach. Happiness will not come if all men try to be saints, or if government, or public opinion, tries to make them. Theocratic government would reduce the possibility of happiness: so would a society, like the one in which Mill lived, where pressure to conform is more extensive than the pressure permitted by Mill's injunctions. Abstractly put, Mill's statements seem innocuously libertarian: when confronted with the positions they exclude, they look like the brisk resolution of an ancient difficulty.

The difficulty Mill attempts to resolve is the difficulty which accompanies realization of the fact that what is meant when one society uses *right* or *reasonable* or *rational* is not what is meant when other societies use these words; that there is, in other words, variation between normative opinions. Some philosophers resolve the contradiction by ignoring it: some suggest that

[1] *Op. cit.*, p. 145.
[2] *Op. cit.*, p. 142.

disagreement is unavoidable whilst temporal existence lasts. Mill, like Plato, Marx and some others, implies that men do really (or would in practice if they could be educated to) agree about the character of the means suitable to determining the content of right action, and that education ought ideally to remove all those blinkers which prejudice, interest, ignorance and animal passion impose on the motives of rational men. Mill assumes that homogeneity will emerge amongst rational men, so long as account is taken of the circumstances: that, if only men will submit their actions to critical examination, a moral, social and intellectual consensus will eventually supersede the miscellaneity of the age in which he lived. Agreement must not be imposed: about that Mill is certain. But agreement about methods of proceeding *will* emerge once moral argument has stimulated the search for basic, fundamental, first principles, and when, 'by the improvement of education, the feeling of unity with our fellow-creatures shall be (. . . what Christ intended it to be) as deeply rooted in our character . . . as the horror of crime in an ordinarily well-brought-up young person'.[1] Antagonistic modes of thought are necessary on the road to Truth: Mill does not always suppose that Truth will be reached. He does claim, however, that one way of approaching Truth is better than others: the injunction to submit preferences to the test of *reason* is, given the meaning he attaches to the word, an invitation to subject the practical judgement to a new manner of reaching political decisions. In a 'regenerated society' where 'scientific education' is more widely diffused 'among the whole people' than hitherto, the deference shown to 'the nearly universal verdict of instructed minds . . . would not be the blind submission of dunces to men of knowledge, but the intelligent deference

[1] [J. S. Mill,] *Utilitarianism* [(1863), ed. Plamenatz, Oxford 1949, pp. 189–90.]

34

of those who know much to those who know still more.'[1] Nor would it be necessary to establish what Comte wanted—'a Spiritual Power . . . a moral and intellectual authority charged with the duty of guiding men's opinions . . . an agency set apart for obtruding upon all classes of persons through the whole of life, the paramount claims of the general interest and the comprehensive ideas that demonstrate the mode in which human actions promote or impair it'.[2] Centralized institutions of this sort are, in Mill's view, dangerous because they are potentially despotic. They are, also, unnecessary. Mill certainly believed 'this salutary ascendancy over opinion should be exercised by the most eminent thinkers': but, if it *were* to be established, it would be established, he thought, not because 'there is an Academy of Sciences or a Royal Society issuing decrees or passing resolutions', but because 'the unanimity is attained without which [this ascendancy] is neither desirable nor possible'.[3]

Education, therefore, is central because it promulgates the general principles by which vocational skills and professional competence should be guided. Education for Mill means general culture: general culture involves propagation of those sorts of influential opinion which constitute the basic commitment of the society in which they are enunciated. General culture is maintained, not by the clergy, who are no longer intellectually pre-eminent, but by the more extensive body of the learned everywhere. As the number of the educated is increased, the respect felt by the unlearned for the opinions of their intellectual betters will increase equally. The agency of authority will be the urge to rationalize and systematize, to ask why a man believes what he thinks he believes: once existing creeds are subjected to rational

---

[1] *Comte and Positivism*, pp. 97–8.   [2] *Op. cit.* pp. 95–6.
[3] *Op. cit.*, p. 98.

systematization, the superiority of the higher minds will impose on the outcome a disinterested utilitarianism. Mill assumes that there is a rational morality and rational ethic to which the higher minds can make an approach: he asserts that it is their business to propagate understanding of the means of approaching it: and he attributes to education, not in school and university only but everywhere else, the task of persuading people who, when they think rationally, want to be persuaded to it.

This view of the importance of education is, in Mill's hands, no more disjointed than his view of the importance of critical self-examination. Education, no less than the self-conscious ethic, is connected with the principle of utility. 'Next to selfishness' he writes 'the principle cause which makes life unsatisfactory is want of mental cultivation'.[1] Just as rational reflection will produce agreement amongst rational men about the methods suitable in searching for truth, so education through general culture is justified by its tendency to produce, and be dominated by, the higher minds. Domination by the higher minds, far from being, in Mill's view, hostile to the principle of utility, is essential to it. The principle of utility does not mean merely that 'actions are right so far as they tend to produce happiness', though it does mean that. The principle of utility means that a calculus exists which imputes to the higher intellectual pleasures the capacity to produce greater happiness than the lower ones: and that the relative value of the various pleasures must be measured by those who, because they have cultivated the intellectual ones, can compare the felicific value of these with the felicific value of others. The importance, and consistency, of Mill's position at this point is great. His criticism of

[1] *Utilitarianism*, p. 176.

Bentham involves not merely the assertion that some pleasures—the pleasure of poetry, for example—are higher than others, or give a greater *amount* of pleasure: it involves the assertion that only men who have experienced both sorts of pleasure have authority to measure the desirability, or felicific value, of the higher. From this follows the assumption that 'the only thing which can justify reckoning one person's opinion as equivalent to more than one is individual mental superiority,'[1] that 'the higher minds' should set the tone of the society in which they live; and hence that *their* sort of education in general culture must be propagated as extensively as possible.

Connected with this elevated view of the function of a free society, is a belief that the binding utilitarian injunction is to maximize, not just the happiness of the individual, 'but the greatest amount of happiness altogether'. Not only is the individual obliged to act so as to produce 'the greatest amount of happiness altogether': between maximizing his own happiness and maximizing happiness altogether, he has to remain absolutely impartial. It is not adequate, and where there is conflict it is wrong, for an individual to prefer *his* happiness to that of society as a whole. In pursuing his own happiness, he may, of course, be increasing the greatest amount of happiness altogether: where this is the case, he need not hesitate to maximize his own. Disinterestedness and impartiality are not, in spite of Comte, the only motives by which a man should feel bound. Nevertheless, disinterestedness and impartiality *are* overriding injunctions: between his own happiness and the happiness of others, impartiality *is* an obligation. This disinterested posture—a fundamental consequence of the principle of utility—is, furthermore, a fundamental consequence of

[1] *Representative Government*, p. 217.

the tendency to submit social action to the test of reason. Disinterestedness, like the self-conscious ethic, is central to Mill's practical doctrine, and tends in the same direction. The sinister influences which make men prefer their own interests, and the interests of their class, to the interests of others (when it is wrong to do so), flourish in the same soil as the unreasoning prejudices that are connected in Mill's mind with the despotism of custom. It is the business of the clerisy, a function of the intellectual élite, to provide (through general culture and education) a systematic indoctrination with a view to freeing men from the habitual arbitrariness which prevents them seeing their social duties for what they are. Once men have grasped the obligation to disinterestedness, their sense of social participation will increase. Each class suffers the temptation to pursue *its* happiness instead of the greatest amount of happiness: each class, so far as it succumbs, is involved in an arbitrary, sinister, selfish limitation of its obligation to fulfil the destinies of rational men. All existing societies are involved in the various sorts of arbitrariness: no society is entirely free. 'The rough method of settling the labourer's share of the produce, the competition of the market, may [in present conditions]', for example, 'represent a practical necessity', but it is 'certainly not a moral ideal'. The ideal at which men should aim is to 'regard working for the benefit of others as a good in itself . . . [to] desire it for its own sake, and not for the sake of remuneration . . . [and to regard] the moral claim of anyone in regard to the provision for his personal wants . . . not [as] a question of *quid pro quo* in respect to his co-operation, but of how much the circumstances of society permit to be assigned to him, consistently with the just claims of others'. This is 'the true moral and social idea of Labour'; 'until labourers and employers perform the work of industry in the spirit in which soldiers perform that of an army, industry will never be moralized, and military life will remain, what, in spite of the anti-social character of its direct object, it has hitherto been—the chief school of moral co-operation'.[1]

Utility to Mill, therefore, means, not just the pursuit of any sort of happiness but disinterested pursuit of the greatest amount of happiness possible—and of that higher happiness, especially, which comes from moral altruism on the one hand and intellectual cultivation on the other. This should be the overriding motive in social action—the achievement of utility considered as a comprehensive description of the interests of man as a progressive and cultivated being, thirsting for elevation of sentiment and voyaging after Truth. It is also the ground on which the cohesiveness of Mill's desire for justice is based. Chapter V of *Utilitarianism* is an attempt to show that justice, like all other social ends, may be subsumed under the heading of Utility, that the desire for justice is a desire for Utility. General Utility enjoins desire for the highest things: justice is hostile to anything which hinders maximization of them. If, in Mill's writing, there is commitment to erode existing social conventions, there is no attempt to erode society altogether. Mill wishes to replace one sort of society by another: but he has no doubt about the need to be tough at the point at which society's existence is in danger. Nor is there uncertainty about the sanctions society ought to impose on men who endanger it. In few places does Mill speak well of the instincts or the animal feelings. But, in maintaining society and a sense of social solidarity, the animal instincts play a full moral part. Mill's view of punishment is as stern as Bentham's, and for Bentham's reasons. Whatever the specific content of

[1] *Comte and Positivism*, pp. 148–9.

utility in Mill's writing—whether the happiness enjoined is of an animal or an elevated sort—there can be no doubt of the benefit to individual happiness which comes from security and the assurance of being defended against assaults on the regular well-being characteristic of stable societies.

The desire for justice takes the form of a desire to punish persons who have done harm, so long as there is a definite person to whom harm has been done. Justice is distinguished from morality by the existence of definite social obligation. It presupposes a 'rule of conduct and a sentiment which sanctions the rule'. The rule 'must be supposed common to all mankind and intended for its good'. The sentiment is a desire that 'punishment may be suffered by those who infringe the rule'; the desire to see justice done, i.e. to punish a wrongdoer, is 'a spontaneous outgrowth from two sentiments—both . . . natural and . . . resembling instincts; the impulse of self-defence, and the feeling of sympathy'.[1]

The feeling ought not, however, to be indiscriminate in its operation. Men tend naturally to resent *any* action that is disagreeable: but the fact that an action is disagreeable is not by itself a ground for inflicting punishment. What makes the feeling acceptable, in a properly regulated society, is that, 'when moralized by the social feeling, it only acts in the directions conformable to the general good'.[2] When we say that a person has a right to anything, 'we mean that he has a valid claim on society to protect him in the possession of it either by the force of law or by that of education and opinion', and the reason why men want *him* to be protected (on grounds of general utility) is because they want to be protected in their own rights also.[3] This sentiment, which we may

[1] *Utilitarianism*, p. 214.   [2] *Op. cit.*, p. 215.
[3] *Op. cit.*, p. 217.

call the sentiment of social solidarity, is not a mild, general benevolence. On the contrary

it has not a rational [element] only, but also an animal element, the thirst for retaliation: and this thirst derives its intensity, as well as its moral justification, from . . . the . . . important and impressive kind of utility . . . concerned . . .—the interest of . . . security. . . . This most indispensable of all necessaries, after physical nutriment, cannot be had, unless the machinery . . . is kept unintermittedly in active play. Our notion therefore of our claim we have on our fellow creatures to join in making safe for us the very groundwork of our existence . . . assumes that character of absoluteness, that apparent infinity and in-commensurability with all other considerations, which constitute the distinction between the feeling of right and wrong and that of ordinary expediency and inexpediency.[1]

It is in this setting and against this background that Mill's doctrine about liberty must be viewed. His detailed delimitation of the power of society (and government) in relation to the individual is made, not in view of the natural right of individuals to be free, but from regard to the consequence to the general interest of imposing limitations on the exercise of social pressure to conform. For natural rights Mill had as much dislike as Bentham. Pursuit of individual liberty for Mill is not, by itself and without regard to its consequences, a proper end of social action. Individuals must be left as free as possible from social pressure, not because they have a *right* to consideration of this sort, but because, if they are not left free, society may find it more difficult than other-wise to achieve the ends for which it exists. Individual freedom must be maximized, not because diversity of opinion is desirable in itself, but because, without diver-sity of opinion, men are unlikely to approach nearer to truth than they have done hitherto. What Mill means by truth is a question that requires investigation:

[1] *Op. cit.*, pp. 217–18.

whatever he means, it is this, and not individual liberty, which he regards as the important objective of human endeavour. The demand for liberty is not the assertion of a fundamentally binding end, but the designation of a means to the end—the end of allowing men to approach as close as possible to that highest of all pleasures which comes from mental cultivation of the closest approximation possible to knowledge of what is True. Liberty is desirable because it is only when conflict of opinion is allowed free play that all free minds are able, in unison with all others, to feel a common sense of participation in the search for the Kingdom of Truth. Mill does not claim that adoption of the positive, scientific method will produce immediate unanimity in the social sciences. 'The method of a science is not the science itself' he says in criticism of Comte.[1] In sociology, where 'the facts [are] more complicated, ... depend ... on a greater concurrence of forces' and are involved 'to an infinitely greater extent [than in other sciences] in personal or class interests and predilection', 'the hope of such accordance of opinion among sociological inquirers as would obtain, in mere deference to their authority, the universal assent which M. Comte's scheme of society requires, must be adjourned to an indefinite distance'.[2] It is not the case that 'when the positive [as distinct from the theological or metaphysical] method which has raised up real sciences on other subjects of knowledge is similarly employed on this, divergence would at once cease'. Matters are not so far advanced: 'the new synthesis is barely begun': 'an unknown duration' must be expected of 'hard thought and violent controversy'.[3] Nevertheless, when the period of conflict *has* passed, Mill supposes that 'a time such as M. Comte

[1] *Comte and Positivism*, p. 120.   [2] *Op. cit.*, pp. 120–1.
[3] *Op. cit.*, p. 120.

reckoned upon *may* come' and 'unless something stops the progress of human improvement, is sure to come'.[1]

Mill, then, is offering persuasion, not to a vulgarly libertarian position, but to a unitary ethic, based on a unitary noetic, which assumes neither that methods of right reasoning are various and diverse, nor that there will be ultimate divergence about its injunctions. It assumes, on the contrary, that, given liberty to reflect and freedom from pressure of mediocrity, the higher minds will use their liberty (and the lower minds, perhaps, even theirs) to play their part in establishing a disinterestedly utilitarian ethic which will have been validated by agreed philosophical procedures. The content of the ethic is a good deal less specific than is sometimes supposed: the type of moral character involved a good deal more uncertain. But of one thing there can be no doubt—in the area in which individuals should be left free to cultivate their motives, the principle of utility will cover *all* the good ends to which rational consideration should make men want to move: and the combination of liberty, utility and general culture is a Revelation-case into which is stuffed *everything* that ought, in Mill's view, to be desired by sensible men.

The political positions for which Mill is famous— delimiting the power of government and asserting the need to maintain a high degree of individual social freedom—are characteristic preoccupations of his writing at all times throughout his life. They are, however, as we have attempted to show, not his chief preoccupations: nor do they represent the central principle from which other positions follow. The central principle is the principle of utility put in the broad manner in which Mill puts it, and having the moral and ethical overtones with which he surrounds it. The principle

[1] *Ibid.*

may also be called the principle of liberty: but it is a sort of spiritual, moral and rational liberty more extensive than the libertarianism for which Mill's doctrine is sometimes mistaken. The doctrine is less practically libertarian in implication than is often supposed, since Mill assumes that, given as wide a freedom as possible to exercise rational choice and taking this freedom as the means, the end will be achieved, not of diversity of opinion pure and simple, but of diversity of opinion within the limits of a rationally homogeneous, agreed, social consensus about the method of judging and the right end to be approached. In considering Mill's specific political injunctions, it is necessary, therefore, to distinguish the instrumental liberties from the ultimate consensus: though, once the distinction is made, it is legitimate to examine the character of the consequences which flow from commitment to pursue the ultimate, general objective.

Mill, as we have said, is concerned less to delimit the province of government than to maximize the opportunities open to citizens to use their practical energies for common purposes. He is irritated by 'impatient reformers' who advocate social improvement through extensive governmental intervention, when they ought to be pursuing the implications of the primary need to get 'possession . . . of the intellects and dispositions of the public'.[1] A good deal of what Mill wished, as a zealous utilitarian, to make government do, had in fact been done by the time he wrote *On Liberty* and *Representative Government*. Mill was, in practical political matters, in spite of his critical pessimism, on a good many winning sides. He changed his view of Comte and Comte's Spiritual Power. But his view of the purpose of governmental intervention was consistent throughout his life.

[1] *Principles*, p. 795.

44

At its most libertarian Mill's view of the *purpose* is the same as his view when it is least so. There is no reason to think he would have dissented in 1868, 1858 or 1838 from the opinion expressed at the end of *Principles of Political Economy* in 1848 that 'government aid, when given merely in default of private enterprise, should be so given as to be as far as possible a course of education for the people in the art of accomplishing great objects by individual energy and voluntary co-operation'.[1]

His opinions about the duties of government are consistent, not just with general expediency, but with his general moral preoccupation. When government intervenes, it should do so in order to maximize utility, whether by ensuring security, increasing liberty or diminishing inequality: but the vagueness of Mill's general injunction leaves government a wide area of permissible activity. He distinguishes between, on the one hand, those areas of governmental activity in which government *has* to act because no one else can, or because no one else can maintain the necessary regularity; and, on the other, those areas in which, although governmental activity ought to be reduced as much as possible, it is necessary, when the public does not manage competently without assistance, that government should act for it. The basic governmental functions have to be performed by government because, if government did not perform them, the social union would degenerate, and general utility be damaged. These necessary activities are connected with Taxation, Land and Property Laws and with the enforcement of justice. In this area there is no alternative to governmental agency: at this point laisser-faire has to be abandoned. In no other area, however, is it essential to abandon it. In general the principle of laisser-faire ought, where

<hr>

[1] *Principles*, p. 978.

possible, to be followed: where local circumstances or temporary conditions make laisser-faire unsuitable, government should manage its intervention with a view to re-establishing the principle as soon as possible. Laisser-faire is the right principle to follow, partly because whatever government does could almost always be done better by private agency, partly because participation in economic activity is a necessary element in the education of the people. For this reason an important economic duty of government is to maintain the operation of the laws, and challenge, of the market economy; land, inheritance and insolvency laws, for example, which hamper free exchange of property should be altered.

However, if Mill's first economic injunction encourages governmental activity chiefly in order to make it unnecessary, his advice does not stop short (where individuals or governments are concerned) at advocating exclusive pursuit of individual self-interest. Self-interest appears in Mill as 'merely individual interests', by contrast with the more desirable sort of 'spontaneous action for a collective interest'.[1] Men must not be tied down to doing what suits them individually: they should involve themselves in determining a 'collective interest'. The collective interest, however, must be determined, not by governmental dictate merely, but by the opinion of society as a whole. Where government exercises, in its own hands, a disproportionately great power, or where it has taken exclusive control of an area of human activity, the moral exercise citizens gain from determining the collective interest is lost, and a significant element in the higher cultivation denied to a significant part of the community. Finally, in pursuing the ideal of a society of generally committed citizens, it is essential to reduce the existing disparity between the educational

[1] *Principles*, p. 948

standards of those who are governed, and the educational standards of those who govern. Nothing does greater damage to social solidarity, to the honesty and integrity of government and to general participation than in-equality of educational opportunity. Education is an essential prerequisite to intelligent government: the agents of the higher cultivation have a necessary part to play in it. Existing English government was amateur and dilletante. It could be improved by infusion from the intelligentsia, and Mill was, for this reason, a strong supporter of the Civil Service competitive examination. But, if the Civil Service should be recruited by com-petitive examination, precautions must be taken against drawing *all* the most highly cultivated intellects into government. Nothing would more certainly produce a Spiritual Despotism, or divide government from the people. Mill was anxious, in other words, to give government the benefit of those higher minds which the higher education produces, whilst at the same time avoiding the dangers which flow from replacing an aristocratic élite by an educational one: and he resolves the difficulty as he resolves others, by asserting that, once education has become general, a common respect for intellect will induce throughout society that unforced homogeneity of opinion which existing irrationalities and existing class conflict have hitherto made impossible.

Mill's political writing, then, is dedicated to advocat-ing the establishment of a society in which all opinions are tolerated and the press is free; in which hereditary wealth is not passed on too unequally, and education is compulsory: where women are free from the arbitrary indignities and limitations they suffer at present, and in which, in spite of the moral merit attached to the labour involved in economic competition, society is not neces-sarily committed to indefinite expansion at the expense

47

of solitude, elevation and reflection. The society of which Mill is the utopian advocate is a free society in which as many men as possible have responsibility for their actions, and in which as few as possible are deprived of that economic responsibility which comes from having a share in ownership. In industrial society large-scale factory production has come, and come to stay: but co-operation is necessary, and the industrial worker should be *involved*. At all levels in society, and at all times, men are to be reasoning, arguing, scrutinizing, probing, in order to subject their own lives, and the institutions and conventions by which they are bound, to the most searching practical tests the cultivated reason can devise.

These tests are searching, and the injunctions they produce, extensive and revolutionary. They anticipate renovation, not just of one aspect of social life or another, but of the whole. 'The family . . . as a step out of the merely animal state into the human' has played its part in human history, but dispersion of 'mankind over the earth in single families, each ruled internally, as families now are, by a patriarchal despot' does nothing to advance 'any community of interest or necessary mental communion, with other human beings'.[1] Mill is not specific about what he wants done to the family, but it is clear that he wants something done in order to break down the control it exercises over individuals. Similarly where women are concerned. Their condition is arbitrary and irrational, their social and legal dependence a 'flagrant social injustice',[2] their status evidence of a 'mouldering fabric of monopoly and tyranny'.[3] 'The ideas and institutions by which the accident of sex is made the groundwork of an inequality of legal rights and a forced dissimilarity of social functions must ere

[1] *Principles*, p. 763.　　　　　　　[2] *Op. cit.*, p. 759.
[3] *Representative Government*, p. 224.

48

long be recognised as the greatest hindrance to moral, social and even intellectual improvement'. Emancipation would not just help check population increase: it would put an end to conditions which, 'by devoting one-half of the human species to [reproduction], . . . making it fill the entire life of one sex, and interweav[ing] itself with almost all the objects of the other [have nursed] the animal instinct in question . . . into the disproportionate preponderance which it has hitherto exercised in human life'.[1]

The outcome of this process, the final consequence of these ameliorative injunctions will be to reduce the dominion of the sexual instinct, mitigate the operation of the acquisitive instinct, break down differences between peoples and ages and races, destroy the effectiveness of dogmatic religion, end the isolation of the family, replace domination in industry by industrial co-operation, and, by extending the interests men have, and the commitments they feel, to the nations in which they live, to develop a general altruistic concern for the well-being of the whole world. Concern is to be directed, not at this nation or that, not at Peking alone or London,[2] but at 'the Grand Etre, Humanity or Mankind . . . including those animal races which enter into real society with man, which attach themselves to him, and voluntarily co-operate with him, like the noble dog who gives his life for his human friend and benefactor'.[3]

That the ennobling power of this grand conception may have its full efficacy . . . the unworthy members of it are best dismissed from our habitual thoughts; and the imperfections which adhered through life, even to those of the dead who deserve honourable remembrance, should be no further borne in mind than is necessary not to falsify our conception of facts; . . . and when reflection, guided by history, has taught us the intimacy

[1] *Principles*, pp. 759–60.   [2] Cf. *On Liberty*, p. 16.
[3] *Later Speculations of M. Comte*, pp. 136–7.

of the connection of every age of humanity with every other, making us see in the earthly destiny of mankind the playing out of a great drama, or the action of a prolonged epic, all the generations of mankind become indissolubly united into a single image, combining all the power over the mind of the idea of Posterity, with our best feelings towards the living world which surrounds us, and towards the predecessors who have made us what we are.[1]

---

[1] *Op. cit.*, pp. 137 and 136.

CHAPTER 3

THE PROOF OF THE DOCTRINE

Society is to be a society, in other words, of seekers after
a cultivated disinterestedness of character and cultivated
elevation of mind, and Mill's work is dedicated on one
view to explaining *how*. It is dedicated, on another, to
explaining *why* society should be deflected in this direction, and on what authority it should be taken that Mill's
direction is the right one. Mill was not content simply
to make practical commitment without argument or
reason. Mill, more than most English philosophers,
displays a desire not just to take his stand and offer his
advice, but also to provide reasons why his advice should
be taken. It is not the present writer's view that Mill's
proof of his practical commitment had binding authority:
but if we are to enter into the spirit of his work, we must
understand what sort of statement he supposed was
possible about it.

In considering these statements, one is conscious of
contradiction. In *Utilitarianism* Mill says, first of all, that
the assertion that all action should be guided by utility
is an assertion for which proof in 'the ordinary and
popular meaning of the term' is impossible.[1] With that
statement, as will become clear later, the present writer
agrees. However, if the principle of utility is not, at this
point in Mill's writing, supposed to be capable of proof,
Mill rejects the idea that 'its acceptance or rejection
must depend on blind impulse or arbitrary choice'.[2] It
is not clear what he means here by 'not arbitrary'.
Presumably, he means something less than capable of

[1] *Utilitarianism*, p. 166.   [2] *Ibid.*

proof (the sense in which one can verify a scientific hypothesis) but something more than being 'a mere commitment about which general reasoning is unnecessary or undesirable'. 'The subject is within the cognisance of the rational faculty: and neither does that faculty deal with it solely in the way of intuition.' In these circumstances 'considerations may be presented capable of determining the intellect either to give or withhold its assent to the doctrine: and this is equivalent to proof'.[1] Clearly, in Mill's mind, reasoning is possible about the principle of utility; and it is also necessary. 'Customary morality is . . . the only one which presents itself to the mind with the feeling of being *in itself* obligatory: and when a person is asked to believe that this morality *derives* its obligation from some general principle round which custom has not thrown the same halo, the assertion is to him a paradox'.[2] If attempts are made to call on a person 'to *adopt* a standard, or refer morality to any basis on which he has not been accustomed to rest it',[3] then those who make the attempt must provide reasons for obliging him to make the change. Utilitarian moral teachers face a problem which confronts all moralists, though equally 'there is no reason why [the principle of utility] might not have all the sanctions which belong to any other system of morals'.[4] Sanctions, however, are not proof; and one returns to the question—what *proof* have we that pursuit of Mill's sort of happiness is the only desirable one?

Of this, in two famous passages, Mill says, first, that 'the general happiness is desirable' as *an* end because 'each person, so far as he believes it to be attainable, desires his own happiness', then that happiness is desirable as *the* end because men 'never value anything else';

[1] *Utilitarianism*, p. 166. [2] *Op. cit.*, p. 189.
[3] *Ibid.* [4] *Op. cit.*, p. 190.

and about this it is necessary to say a few words. The passage is, in the first place, an attempt to provide an answer to the question: can the *first principles of conduct*, which are as incapable of proof as the first principles of knowledge, nevertheless, like the first principles of knowledge, 'be subject of a direct appeal to the faculties which judge of fact—namely, our senses and our internal consciousness'. 'Can an appeal be made to the same faculties on questions of practical ends? or by what other faculty is cognisance taken of them?'[1] Secondly, this statement is a good deal less than proof of anything because Mill has already annexed to *utility* or *happiness* so comprehensive a content that it does little more than assert that happiness is desirable because men do in fact desire what their higher natures always have desired. This says something: that men do not, for example, value that which disturbs their higher natures, but it says little more. Finally, the formula is inadequate because the explanatory assumption in which it is involved gives an inadequate account of the diversity of human motivation. It is not the case that all, or most, men always, or usually, do desire the higher cultivation at the expense of 'the lower'. Not all men think the pleasure of listening to Weber or Mozart 'higher' than what Mill thinks of as vulgar sensual entertainments: it is no answer to anyone who takes this point of view to say that another man with experience of both has judged that the intellectual pleasures are 'higher'. Whether the standard of judgement is the *amount* or the *quality* of pleasure produced, Mill's explanatory statement rests on unproven assumptions about the validity of inter-personal comparisons between the pleasure given by *his* pleasures to a man who has little intellectual capacity, and the pleasure given by *his* pleasures to a man whose intellectual capacity is

[1] *Op. cit.*, p. 198.

53

greater. Men desire, or think they desire, a great variety of ends: even if it amounted to proof to say that, because all men tend to desire X, therefore X is desirable, the argument would be irrelevant to the problem under discussion—since men do not feel unanimous respect for the end about which Mill is writing.

If, then, Mill's proof of the principle of utility is inadequate, is the principle to be thought of as a commitment about which reasoning can reach no necessary conclusion? For reasons which will become apparent in a moment, the present writer thinks it should be (though he does not, for that reason, think it less adequate as a guide to action). Mill, however, does not treat it in this way; but, before explaining the view the present author takes of its place in Mill's scheme, it is desirable to show what part Mill supposed it to play. Mill's view of the status of his proofs is connected with his view of the status, and possibility, of political sociology. Book VI of *A System of Logic* lays out Mill's assumptions about the connection between politico-sociological explanation on the one hand and the practice of politics on the other. Mill is not, in Book VI, as unambiguous as he might be: nor does he mention the clerisy by name. Nevertheless, he makes clear his belief that philosophers and political sociologists between them have normative political authority and that the indefeasibility of utilitarian principles rests on joint determination by both. Mill's argument at this point is difficult to disentangle. The technical character of Book VI does not, however, obscure the claim that philosophers and sociologists, by reason of their explanatory competence, have normative authority also, and that they should, at the point at which injunctions are delivered, perform some of the functions performed by politicians, preachers and citizens in general. Sociology, therefore, is central to the questions we are discussing in this chapter; it is to consideration of it that attention must now be turned.

(i)

Mill claimed, in the preface to *A System of Logic*, that 'the concluding Book [Book VI] is an attempt to contribute towards the solution of a question, which the decay of old opinions, and the agitation that disturbs European society to its inmost depths, render as important in the present day to the practical interests of human life, as it must at all times be to the completeness of our speculative knowledge: viz. Whether moral and social phenomena are really exceptions to the general certainty and uniformity of the course of nature; and how far the methods, by which so many of the laws of the physical world have been numbered among truths irrevocably acquired and universally assented to, can be made instrumental to the formation of a similar body of received doctrine in moral and political science.'[1] One objection to the philosophical predominance of Intuitionism was that, by consecrating habitual, instinctive, arbitrary prejudices, it encouraged conservative instincts and 'indolence'. Intuitionism was objectionable, because its doctrines made it difficult to show, as the moral reformer had to show, not only 'that changes [should] be made in things which are supported by powerful and widely-spread feelings' but also 'how these powerful feelings had their origin, and how those facts came to seem necessary and indefeasible'.[2] In the writings of Hamilton, Mansel and Whewell, the form of Intuitionism which Mill chose to attack, tended, according to his account, 'to treat [feelings and moral facts] as ultimate elements of human nature' and to 'discourage the explanation [of them] by

[1] [J. S. Mill: *A*] *System of Logic*, [*Ratiocinative and Inductive* (1843), London 1875, vol. I, p. viii.]
[2] *Autobiography*, p. 273.

circumstances and association'. Whilst affecting to recognize the Relativity of Knowledge, it was 'addicted to holding up favourite doctrines as intuitive truths' and 'deem[ed] intuition to be the voice of Nature and of God, speaking with an authority higher than that of our reason'.[1] By failing to accept the implications of the fact that 'by far the greater part of [the] differences . . . . between individuals, races or sexes' can be explained by 'differences in circumstances', Intuitionism failed to be sensitive to the possibility of 'rational treatment of great social questions', and constituted itself 'one of the greatest stumbling-blocks to human improvement'.[2] The practical influence it had exercised in the previous fifty years meant that Mill supposed himself to be undertaking both a practical and an explanatory task when he battled with the question—on what *philosophical* ground can we claim to subvert the habitual prejudices which, under the dominance of custom and supported by the School of Intuition, are generally taken to have moral and political authority?

Mill opens his account of the problem in Book VI of *A System of Logic* by claiming that he intends to 'rescue . . . the proper study of mankind' from the empiricism to which in practice it has succumbed, and proposes to do this by asking whether the methods which have been successful in discovering the 'laws of many simpler phenomena' (i.e. in the physical sciences) can be applied to moral and political action also.[3] *A System of Logic* is not an attempt to 'construct . . . the sciences of Ethics and Politics'. It is an attempt to ask 'whether moral sciences exist, or can exist: to what degree of perfection they are susceptible of being carried; and which of [the] methods . . . characteristic of science in general are more

[1] *Op. cit.*, pp. 273–4.   [2] *Ibid.*
[3] *System of Logic*, II, p. 418.

especially suited to the various branches of moral enquiry'.[1]

Sociology is taken, initially, to have explanatory functions not normative ones, to show what socio-political activity is like, not what it should become; in approaching it, Mill makes a number of assumptions which constitute the direction of his doctrine. Ethology explains the nature of individual character, and is relevant to Sociology. Sociology indeed rests on the conclusions of Ethology; to understand what sociology can say about the nature of social action, we must understand what Ethology can say about individual character —and in particular about the predictability of human action. 'Given the motives' Mill writes 'which are present to an individual's mind, and given likewise the character and disposition of the individual, the manner in which he will act might be unerringly inferred: [and] . . . if we knew the person thoroughly, and knew all the inducements which are acting upon him, we could foretell his conduct with as much certainty as we can predict any physical event'. Every action is the result of a cause: to know the cause and disposition of the agent, though not to deny the reality of freedom, is to be in a position to predict the outcome of free human actions.[2]

Nevertheless, although actions are determined by causes, a major difficulty confronting the social or moral scientist is the difficulty of discovering them. The study of human nature is not an exact study: although it 'would have attained the ideal perfection of a science if it enabled us to foretell how an individual would think, feel, or act, throughout life . . . nothing approaching to this can be done.'[3] The difficulty in predicting the *whole*

---

[1] *Op. cit.*, p. 419. [2] *Op. cit.*, pp. 422 and 425.
[3] *Op. cit.*, p. 433.

of the circumstances in which an individual will be placed, and the fact that the actions of an individual are the joint outcome of his character *and* the circumstances, means that 'the agencies which determine human character are so numerous . . . that in the aggregate they are never in any two cases exactly similar.'[1] However, 'inasmuch . . . as many of those effects which it is of most importance to render amenable to human foresight and control are determined, like the tides, in an incomparably greater degree by general causes, than by all partial causes taken together . . . it is evidently possible . . . to make predictions which will *almost* always be verified'.[2] These approximate generalizations are only the 'lowest kind of empirical laws' (by which Mill means 'a uniformity . . . which holds true in all instances within our limits of observation').[3] For scientific purposes, they need to be 'resolved into the properties of the causes on which the phenomena depend' and Ethology—the Science of Human Nature—'may be said to exist in proportion as the approximate truths which compose a practical knowledge of mankind can be exhibited as corollaries from the universal laws of human nature on which they rest'.[4]

What, then, is the character and relevance of these 'universal laws of human nature'? They are first of all, 'universal'. Although 'mankind have not one universal character . . . there exist universal laws of the Formation of Character. And since it is by these laws, combined with the facts of each particular case, that the whole of the phenomena of human action and feelings are produced, it is on these that every rational attempt to construct the science of human nature *in the concrete, and for practical purposes,* [my italic] must proceed'.[5] One of the limitations of the psychological and philo-

---

[1] *Op. cit.,* pp. 433–4.   [2] *Op. cit.,* p. 434.   [3] *Op. cit.,* p. 448.
[4] *Op. cit.,* pp. 434–5.   [5] *Op. cit.,* p. 452.

sophical reaction of 'the last and present generation against the philosophy of the eighteenth century' i.e. of Intuitionism, has been the tendency of 'the majority of those who speculate on human nature . . . dogmatically to assume that . . . mental differences . . . among human beings, are ultimate facts incapable of being either explained *or altered*,[1] rather than [to] take the trouble of . . . referring [them] to the outward causes by which they are for the most part produced, and on the removal of which they would cease to exist'.[2] The *instinctive* parts of human character (corresponding to the instincts of animals) cannot be accounted for in this way, but in general, Mill says, differences between individuals can be accounted for by reference to a combination of circumstances, physical characteristics and education: and it is the business of Ethology to provide generalizations which will make this sort of explanation possible. Ethology is an inexact deductive science which will live on corollaries from its experimental counterpart, psychology: it will, when it has come to exist, have both practical and scientific value. It must necessarily be imperfect because the subject-matter is complicated: but it is not, for that reason, futile. It is a distinctly legitimate undertaking, not least, Mill supposes, because it leads into its more extended sister—Sociology, or the 'Science of Society'.

In dealing with the possibility of a 'Science of Society', Mill rejects two accounts of its functions and one criticism sometimes made of its feasibility. The views he rejects are, first, the view that it is an experimental science, and second, the view that it is an abstract one. He rejects the first because it assumes that political science can produce an adequate induction by simple observation and experiment. He rejects this view, partly

---

[1] *My italic.*   [2] *Op. cit.,* p. 446.

59

because he does not believe a real induction possible 'without the assistance of any theory', much more because 'effects which [like political and social effects] depend on a complication of causes [cannot] be made the subject of a true induction by observation and experiment'.[1] Exponents of the Geometrical or Abstract Method in political science, on the other hand, make the opposite error of underestimating the complexity of political practice. Though they are right to reject the possibility of 'establishing by casual observation or direct experimentation, a true theory of sequences so complex as . . . those of the social phenomena',[2] they misunderstand the value of deductive science. Instead of taking Astronomy as the model for the social sciences, they take Geometry—'a science of co-existent facts altogether independent of the laws of the succession of phenomena'.[3] This is inadequate, in Mill's view, because Geometry (unlike Mechanics) does not take account of the 'case of conflicting forces'—with the result that the 'geometrical theory of society' seems to suppose that 'each [social phenomenon] results always from only one force, one single property of human nature'.[4] Social phenomena are, in fact, the result of conflicting forces: accounts which ignore this are inadequate in explanation and imperfect guides to practice. Hobbes' view that society is based on fear, and Bentham's that it is based on interest, were defective for this reason; whilst natural right and contract theory are inadequate because *their* supporters make the more fundamental error of 'treat[ing] an art like a science' [i.e. a practical injunction like an explanatory statement] and imagining that it is possible to have a 'deductive art' based on 'universal precepts' —a body of 'political conclusions', drawn 'not from

[1] *Op. cit.*, pp. 470–1.   [2] *Op. cit.*, p. 479.
[3] *Op. cit.*, pp. 479–80.   [4] *Op. cit.*, p. 480.

laws of nature, not from sequences of phenomena, real or imaginary, but from unbending practical maxims'.[1]

Social science, then, is neither purely experimental nor abstractly deductive. Experimental verification is seldom possible, but verification *a posteriori* almost always is. Social science does not consist only, as Comte thought, in 'generalisations from history' which have been 'verified [but] not originally suggested by deduction from the laws of human nature'[2]: it consists also of deduction *from* the laws of human nature *to* the historical subject-matter. The number of laws which affect the operation of society is not great, but the number of data to which the laws have to be applied, is. In considering actual situations, it is seldom possible to give adequate explanation by isolating the operation of *one* law. There is no reason to suppose that 'even with respect to tendencies, we could arrive . . . at any great number of propositions which will be true in all societies without exception [for] whatever affects, in an appreciable degree, any one element of the social state, affects it through all the other elements'. Since, furthermore, 'we can never either understand in theory or command in practice the condition of a society in any one respect, without taking into consideration its condition in all other respects', it follows that 'we can never . . . affirm with certainty that a cause which has a particular tendency in one people or in one age will have exactly the same tendency in another, without referring back to our premises, and performing over again for the second age or nation, that analysis of the whole of its influencing circumstances which we had already performed for the first'.[3]

All deductive propositions, therefore, are 'hypothetical'; they explain without reference to particular circumstances what *would* happen *if* an element in action

[1] *Op. cit.*, p. 481.　　[2] *Op. cit.*, p. 490.　　[3] *Op. cit.*, pp. 492–3.

were the only operative one. They show, for example, how economic laws *would* operate *if* men pursued economic well-being as their only, or overriding, motive. Men, as political economists know perfectly well, do not do this—or at any rate most men do not: explanation of the condition of any particular society must in these circumstances take account of the laws relevant to all facets of human activity. In these separate hypothetical sciences—of which political economy is an example—the deductive method is suitable. In constructing these sciences, it is legitimate to isolate certain sorts of cause and ask what effects would follow in a uniform set of general conditions. This is a legitimate exercise, a necessary part of Sociology. It is, however, not the whole of Sociology, and by itself would not do much to establish it. If the nature of Society is to be understood, it is necessary to ask not 'what will be the effect of a given cause in a certain state of society', but 'what are the laws which determine [the] general circumstances' within which the laws of the hypothetical sciences operate, 'what [are] the causes which produce, and the phenomena which characterize, States of Society generally', and what are 'the laws according to which any state of society produces the state which . . . takes its place'.[1] This is 'the general science of society'. It is the high point and pivot of Mill's Sociology —the enquiry 'by which the conclusions of the other and more special kind of enquiry must be limited and controlled'.[2]

It is easier to see what Mill takes to be the subject-matter for explanation by general sociology than to see what sort of explanation general sociology would be able to give. The subject-matter is the 'State of Society', and by this is meant 'the simultaneous state of all the

[1] *Op. cit.*, pp. 508–10.   [2] *Op. cit.*, p. 508.

greater social facts or phenomena'.[1] One facet of the investigation is to discover correlations between the different elements in social structures so as to establish that 'when one of the features of society is in a particular state, a state of many other features . . . always or usually coexists with it'.[2] Such uniformities are corollaries from the 'laws of causation by which these phenomena are really determined': they result from 'the laws which regulate the succession between one state of society and another': to establish them is, together with establishment of the 'requisites of the social union', the central task of empirical sociology.[3]

The order of succession between one state of society and another is, however, not a 'law of nature', but an empirical law with relevance so far as observation extends. It cannot, by itself, provide a basis for prediction. For prediction to be possible (and prediction is felt by Mill to be desirable), it is necessary to connect the 'empirical law' with the 'psychological and ethological laws on which it must depend' so that it can, 'by the consilience of deduction *a priori* with historical evidence . . . be converted from an empirical law into a scientific one'.[4] Mill, in a number of places, has sharp words to say about the historical writing of his contemporaries. 'The only check [on the adequacy of historical generalisation]' he says 'is constant verification by psychological and ethological laws': for this reason 'no one but a person competently skilled in those laws is capable of preparing the materials for historical generalisation'. In the England of his day, however, 'history cannot yet be said to be at all cultivated as a science'.[5] Historical generalization lacks sociological authority unless grounds can be produced for it in human nature, though it would

---

[1] *Op. cit.*, p. 508. [2] *Op. cit.*, p. 509. [3] *Op. cit.*, p. 509–10.
[4] *Op. cit.*, p. 512. [5] *Op. cit.*, p. 515.

not be possible, by 'setting out from the principles of human nature and . . . the general circumstances of the position of our species, to determine *a priori* the order in which human development must take place'.[1] Both processes are necessary. As the generations have succeeded one another, the character of each generation has tended less and less to be 'the result of the universal circumstances of the human race', more and more the outcome of 'the qualities produced in us by the whole previous history of humanity'; and if these qualities failed in fact to show any regularity, then general Sociology would be impossible. It happens, however, that 'the natural varieties of mankind, and the original diversities of local circumstances, are much less considerable than the points of agreement' with the consequence that 'a certain degree of uniformity' *can* be discerned 'in the progressive development of the species and . . . its works' —a uniformity which 'tends to become greater . . . as . . . the evolution of each people . . . is gradually brought under the influence, (which becomes stronger as civilisation advances) of the other nations of the earth'.[2]

Some of the results of historical investigation—as, for example, that no society was ever held together without laws, usages, tribunals, organized force or public authority—'although . . . obtained by comparing' and 'amount[ing] in themselves only to empirical laws' may be 'found to follow with so much probability from general laws of human nature that the consilience of the two processes raises the evidence to proof, and the generalisations to the rank of scientific truths'.[3] Once the empirical laws which history provides have been connected with the principles of human nature, and once success has been achieved in combining 'the statical view of social phenomena with the dynamical, consider-

[1] *Op. cit.*, p. 513.   [2] *Op. cit.*, pp. 513–14.   [3] *Op. cit.*, p. 519.

ing not only the progressive changes of the different elements, but the contemporaneous condition of each', then it may be possible to 'obtain empirically the law of correspondence . . . between the simultaneous states . . . [and] the simultaneous changes of [the] elements', and to produce, as a final achievement, when this law of correspondence is subjected to verification, 'the real scientific derivative law of the development of humanity and human affairs'.[1]

This has about it, at first sound, a ring of conclusive generality: but scrutiny reveals three things. The first, about which more will be said in the second section of this book, is that, whatever the language in which he conceals it, Mill is in fact giving an account of the character of historical explanation. He calls the method appropriate to General Sociology the Inverse Deductive or Historical Method: and concludes his account of the Science of Society by remarking that a 'Philosophy of History is generally admitted to be at once the verification and the initial form of the Philosophy of the Progress of Society'.[2] The second elucidation to offer of the nature of the 'real scientific derivative law of the development of humanity and human affairs' is that, whilst recognizing the complexity of human affairs, it assumes that 'one social element . . . is . . . predominant, and almost paramount, among the agents of the social progression . . . the state of the speculative faculties of mankind; including the nature of the beliefs which by any means they have arrived at, concerning themselves and the world by which they are surrounded'.[3] 'Intellectual activity, the pursuit of truth' is not, Mill argues, 'among the more powerful propensities of human nature', but 'all the other dispositions of our nature which contribute to [social] progress [are] dependent on it for the means of

---

[1] *Op. cit.*, p. 525.　　[2] *Op. cit.*, p. 530.　　[3] *Op. cit.*, p. 525.

accomplishing their share of the work'.[1] The history of thought is, therefore, the 'central chain' of human progress: 'every considerable advance in material civilisation has been preceded by an advance in knowledge . . . and any . . . great social change . . . has had for . . . precursor a great change in the opinions and modes of thinking of society'.[2] Emphasis is placed, not on the accidental outcome of the clash of wills on which so much of history depends, but on deliberate human intention supported by purposive ratiocination. Purposive ratiocination is assumed, at this point, to be self-determining. Nor does Mill consider the implications of the view he expresses in relation to Ethology, that thought, so far from being self-determining, is, like everything else, subject to causal influence.

Thirdly, it is necessary to note the strong commitment to belief in the rational unity of the species which characterizes Mill's Sociology. The possibility of sociology depends on the assumption that similarities between persons and societies with different histories are more significant than the differences. Not only is sociology connected with the belief that unity is possible amongst men, it is connected with the assumption that the subject for study—Man in Society—can be successfully pursued only so far as the higher rational impulses, imposing themselves on the lower ones, help to bring this unity about. The more the disinterested impulses prevail, and in prevailing, unify a sort of utilitarian Humanity, the more relevant will Sociology be to the practical problems with which mankind is confronted; the more effectively sociological explanation insists on the importance of this interdependence, the more confidently will the leap be made from the explanatory insistence that interdependence exists to the normative

[1] *Op. cit.*, pp. 525–6. [2] *Op. cit.*, p. 527.

66

claim that sociology validates a preference for disinterested motives. 'As the strongest propensities of uncultivated or half-cultivated human nature (being the
purely selfish ones and those of a sympathetic character
which partake most of the nature of selfishness) evidently
tend . . . to disunite mankind not to unite them—to
make them rivals not confederates; social existence is
only possible by a disciplining of those more powerful
propensities, which consists in subordinating them to a
common system of opinions'.[1]

Sociology, then, is intimately connected with the
Philosophy of History, and with that form of the History
of Thought which imputes to self-conscious rationality a
higher importance in the development of human history
than to unselfconscious action or the operation of unpredictable accident. It is, one might say (though Mill
does not), the stage in political studies which cor-
responds to the stages reached by certain of the natural
sciences and enjoined by Mill's universal liberalism.
One might, with reason, say these things: they would
be important things to have said. And yet to say them
will neither explain Mill's belief in the importance of
the study to which he draws attention, nor convey the coherence of the connection between the scientific authority
of Sociology and the normative injunctions of the Principle of Utility. In order to understand the intimacy of
the connection we must ask, therefore: what normative
claim does Mill make for sociology? what authority do its
statements carry? what relevance are they supposed to
have for the practice of politics?

(ii)

Mill opens his chapters on Sociology by complain-
ing that 'the condition . . . of politics, as a branch of

[1] *Op. cit.*, p. 526.

knowledge, was until very lately, and has scarcely even yet ceased to be, that which Bacon animadverted on, as the natural state of the sciences while their cultivation is abandoned to practitioners; not being carried on as a branch of speculative enquiry, but only with a view to the exigencies of daily practice'.[1] It is, he goes on, in these circumstances not surprising that 'the philosophy of society . . . should contain few general propositions sufficiently precise and certain, for common inquirers to recognise in them a scientific character'; or that there should be 'no hope that [laws of society], though our knowledge of them were as certain and as complete . . . as in astronomy would enable us to *predict* [my italic] the history of society'.[2] However, even if we cannot *predict*,

an amount of knowledge quite insufficient for prediction may be most valuable for guidance, [and] the science of society would have attained a very high point of perfection if it enabled us in any given condition . . . to understand by what causes [society] had, in any and every particular, been made what it was; whether it was tending to any, and to what, changes; what effects each feature of its existing state was likely to produce in the future; *and by what means any of those effects might be prevented, modified, or accelerated, or a different class of effects superinduced* [my italic].

Sociology, in other words, is not just historical: it does not confine itself to explaining how things were, or how they have come to be what they are. Nor is it predictive in the sense merely that it offers explanatory prognostication about what is likely to happen in the future. It offers also advice and guidance about the means most suitable to make things happen. Once its constituent sciences have reached a certain stage of development, Mill is saying, there is no reason why sociology should not offer this sort of guidance. Not only is there no

[1] *Op. cit.*, p. 464.   [2] *Op. cit.*, pp. 465–6.

reason why it should not, there is every reason why it should. To do so would free politicians from the limitations of the empiricism by which they tend to be confined: and a new period in political history could begin. The method, the Inverse Deductive or Historical Method, culminating in the Philosophy of History, is the necessary instrument of this achievement: once the method is used on the material men have to hand,

we may hereafter succeed not only in looking far forward into the future history of the human race [but may also] determin[e] what artificial means may be used, and to what extent to accelerate the natural progress in so far as it is beneficial; to compensate for . . . its inherent inconveniences . . . and to guard against the dangers or accidents to which our species is exposed from the necessary incidents of its progression. Such practical instructions [Mill concludes] founded on the highest branch of speculative sociology, will form the noblest and most beneficial portions of the Political Art.[1]

Now were Mill saying only that if, in any given circumstances, men want to achieve a given end, then they must take account of what they know about the nature of politics and society, it would be impossible to disagree. It might be possible to doubt whether systematically *written* knowledge would be more useful than the experience of politicians: one might accuse Mill of a certain arrogance in supposing that it would. It might be doubted whether the high generality claimed for sociological laws would facilitate prediction, or, if it did, whether ability to predict might not make normative decision unnecessary. It might seem, also, if thought *is* subject to causal action, that the self-determining character of thought, and its central significance in human history, would be undermined. If it were undermined,

---

[1] *Op. cit.*, p. 529.

the significance of moral and political choice might be reduced and the normative authority of reflective philosophy diminished. Critical reflection is clearly of first importance to Mill, but there is a tendency to base the indefeasibility of utilitarian principles on the prediction (irrelevant to normative judgement) that disinterestedness will in fact prevail. These things are far from clear. What is clear is that if Mill's sociology were a value-free undertaking, or a purely explanatory one, its explanatory predictions could be used to advance any objective that might be thought desirable. If that were all Mill wished to imply, he would have maintained the distinction he thinks he has drawn between explanation and injunction; and we must look closely at the final chapter of *A System of Logic* to see how far he does.

When one looks at Chapter XII—*Of the Logic of Practice or Art including Morality and Policy* one finds, first of all, unambiguous statement of the distinction between practice and explanation. 'The imperative mood' he writes 'is the characteristic of art as distinguished from science. Whatever speaks in rules, or precepts, not in assertions respecting matters of fact, is art': and 'the Method . . . of . . . Ethics [and also of political policy] can be no other than that of Art, or Practice, in general'.[1] This seems clear, and, at first sight, reasonable. However, although 'art' is distinguished from 'science', and the 'art of policy' from the 'science of society', it is asserted, nevertheless, that there is close connection between them. In political practice (or art) a great many decisions are taken not, as a judge's decisions normally are, according to rules, but according to reasons: a legislator who habitually takes decisions 'by rules rather than by their reasons . . . is rightly', Mill says, 'judged to be a mere pedant and the slave of his formulas'.[2] And if, as Mill

<hr>

[1] *Op. cit.*, p. 546.   [2] *Op. cit.*, p. 547.

thinks, it is necessary, in order to act rightly, to have the right reasons for acting, we may ask what sort of reasons Mill takes to be relevant.

In answering this question, we reach the point at which the connection between practice and explanation is closest. For

'the reasons of a maxim of policy, or of any other rule of art, can be no other than the theorems of the corresponding science ... The art proposes to itself an end to be attained, defines the end, and hands it over to the science [which] receives it, considers it as a phenomenon ... to be studied and ... sends it back to art with a theorem of the combination of circumstances by which it could be produced'.[1]

Art does no more than supply 'the original major premise which asserts that the attainment of the given end is desirable' but, once it has done that, the practical authority of science is great. It is of course not always conclusive: 'the [scientific] theorem or speculative truth is not ripe for being turned into a precept, until the whole and not a part merely, of the operation which belongs to science, has been performed'.[2] If 'a rule of art' is based on a less than comprehensive scientific statement, it will follow that 'whenever any counteracting cause, overlooked by the theorem, takes place, the rule will be at fault: we shall employ the means and the end will not follow'.[3] For practical purposes 'rules must be formed from something less than ... ideally perfect theory; in the first place because the theory can seldom be made ideally perfect; and next, because, if all the counteracting contingencies ... were included, the rules would be too cumbrous'. For this reason 'in the complicated affairs of life, and still more in those of states and societies, rules cannot be relied on without constantly referring back to the scientific laws on which they are

[1] *Op. cit.*, pp. 547–8.   [2] *Op. cit.*, p. 548.   [3] *Ibid.*

71

founded'.[1] They are, therefore, 'provisional': 'they do not at all supersede the propriety of going through (when circumstances permit) the scientific process requisite for framing a rule from the data of the particular case before us'.[2] The rule has to be specific, not universal; rules of this sort are not 'rules of conduct generally'.[3] Nevertheless, when all these limitations are taken into account, these rules may be expected to provide a body of specific, authoritative, binding advice about the way in which, in order to achieve the objects which ought to be achieved, 'it would be least perilous to act'.

The question, then, is, how do men know that something *should be*? The fact that someone approves an end is no sufficient reason why other people should approve it. Nor is widespread assent a reason for assenting either. Reasons must be given: for purposes of practice 'every one must be required to justify his approbation' by reference to 'general premises, determining what are the proper objects of approbation, and what the proper order of precedence among those objects'.[4] This is a necessary part of the approach to right living, and 'the most elaborate . . . exposition of the laws of succession and co-existence . . . will be of no avail towards the art of Life or of Society if the ends to be aimed at . . . are left to the vague suggestions of the *intellectus sibi permissus* or . . . taken for granted without analysis or questioning'.[5]

In order to know how to live rightly, then, Mill is saying, it is essential to have not only habitual commitment but also a 'complete doctrine of Teleology',[6] which has to be articulately enunciated and referred to, not relegated to the area of unargued assumption. Just as there is a *philosophia prima* peculiar to Science, so 'there

---

[1] *Op. cit.*, p. 549. [2] *Ibid.* [3] *Op. cit.*, p. 550.
[4] *Op. cit.*, p. 553. [5] *Op. cit.*, p. 554. [6] *Ibid.*

is a Philosophia Prima peculiar to Art . . . [a body] of first principles of Conduct . . . [a] standard by which to determine the goodness or badness, absolute and comparative, of ends, or objects of desire'[1]; and it is the business of the philosopher to establish it. Mill, in criticizing Intuitionism, is emphatic about the fact that 'whatever that standard is, there can be but one', and adduces the general consensus amongst non-intuitionist moralists to support the assertion. The fact that there is *one*, and not many, makes it possible definitely to graduate ends, or purposes, and at this point one expects Mill to graduate his.

It would be foolish to criticize Mill for failing to do what he was not, in *A System of Logic*, trying to do: one ought not to make too much of the fact that he does not there provide any justification of the Principle of Utility. He says, indeed, explicitly that proof will be found elsewhere. We have looked at *Utilitarianism* and found the proof wanting: though that is not to say that something might not have been found if *Utilitarianism* had been a better, or earlier, book. Nevertheless, when one reads, on page 559 of *A System of Logic*, assertion of the overriding merit of the principle, a certain abruptness seems to have intervened. Mill is affecting to argue that there is a *philosophia prima*, a body of principles of which 'for purposes of practice everyone must be required to justify his approbation': but it is difficult to see anything more than unargued commitment in the statement that 'without attempting in this place to justify my opinion, or even to define the kind of justification which it admits of, I merely declare my conviction, that the general principle to which all rules of practice ought to conform, and the test by which they should be tried, is that of conduciveness to the happiness of mankind, or rather, of all

[1] *Ibid.*

73

sentient beings: in other words that the promotion of happiness is the principle of Teleology'. There is elucidation of the character of the principle in the page that follows and in *Utilitarianism*: in one sense, the whole of Mill's writing is an attempt to indicate the sort of action to which his interpretation of the principle makes him wish to persuade his readers. But if it is proof we are looking for (and in this chapter it is) then it must be answered that, in place of argument we have assertion, and that, what might be supposed to fulfil the function of demonstration is in fact declaration of faith in the future. This would not be of great importance if Mill knew what he had done, or if commitment did not uncritically permeate the advice offered both by Sociology and by the *philosophia prima* of practice. A defender of Mill might point out that Mill knew perfectly well that he does not *prove* his commitments, and that *A System of Logic* justifies this sort of omission. A critic might reply that whatever justification *A System of Logic* provides, it does not justify Mill's certainty. The critic might add that Mill's commitment to disinterestedness is sustained by uncritically taking the (sensible) explanatory definition that morality arises because no man can live by considering himself alone, and inflating it into the injunction (which does not at all follow) that men ought always to be acting in more or less self-conscious awareness of their debts to others. The critic might conclude that, for a writer who attaches such great significance to critical self-examination, Mill is uncritical and unselfconscious at precisely the point at which the demand for proof might be least convenient. For if, as he supposes, 'all other arts are subordinate [to the] Art of Life' and if the Art of Life *'which, in the main, is unfortunately still to be created'*, is 'a joint result of laws of nature disclosed by science, and of the general principles of . . . Teleology,

74

or . . . Doctrine of Ends',[1] then Teleology, Philosophy and Political Sociology together are taken to have a normative power for which no justification is offered.

We conclude, then, that behind the caution, subtlety and critical awareness of the difficulties inherent in the pretensions he is maintaining, Mill is saying that Political Philosophy and Political Sociology have power to establish a body of explanation of the character of social action with relevance and authority, not just for explanatory activity, but as the base on which moral and political motive must be grounded. Mill is neither uncritical nor stupid at this point, and there is a sense (though not one he is concerned to stress) in which what he is saying *is* an explanation of what all men do. Everyone *has* a body of truths, assumptions about the character of society and beliefs about the range of possibility open to political action, which *does* determine what he thinks it feasible to maintain as a practical political purpose. Few men—certainly no politicians of any experience—will readily commit themselves in private to policies to which they *know* the circumstances make it impossible to give effect. About this there is unlikely to be dispute: though to say this is not to say much. Mill, however, is saying a great deal more. The claim to rescue political science from 'empiricism' must be seen in conjunction with his view of the scientific importance of the clerisy. For if each Art, or body of Practice, rests on a parallel body of explanation, if it is a function of the clerisy to propagate this body of explanation, and if the Art of Life (including the Art of Politics) has, after two thousand years of continuous European history, only just begun to be formulated, then the authority, and responsibility, of the clerisy in practice in the future will clearly be impressive. What each

[1] *Op. cit.*, p. 553.

75

generation takes to be explanatory truth makes *some* impact on practice, but no one should want, without the closest scrutiny, to attribute to those who offer political explanation normative authority more extensive than this. It is reasonable to assert, in explanation, that disinterestedness is connected with all moral decision, but to establish this does not establish the injunction that disinterested motives are the right motives to have. There is a great gap between offering, with a certain sceptical modesty, as relevant to political conduct, explanatory statements which are admittedly rough, and difficult to verify, and which cannot always take account of the circumstances in which action is involved, and the claim that normative authority is dependent on them. We must not reject the whole of Mill's position in exposing the philosophical irrelevance of a part. But it is important to be clear that Mill is making a brisk, brash, agitated plea for the supersession of one style of politics by another. Too often, beneath the confident academic manner, his criticisms of mid-nineteenth-century aristocratic government, reveal hostility to *all* its conventions, irritation at the fact that its language was not the language of the higher intelligentsia, and a desire, foreign to all explanatory concerns, radically to renovate it.

CHAPTER 4

LIBERALISM AND
THE RELIGION OF HUMANITY

The position we are maintaining is that Mill's fundamental principles have neither proof nor philosophical
authority, but are commitments to action, the outcome
of assertions to claim knowledge of the nature of the
world and the direction men's duty ought to take within
it: and that they cannot sustain claims to be something
other, or something more, than this. Mill seems sometimes to suggest that they perform one function—a
philosophical, or even a positive, scientific one—but at
times that they perform the other, practical one. He does
not always think that they have scientific authority: at
moments when he is most explicit, he does not say so at
all. Nevertheless, where assumptions are made without
scrutiny, he seems to think it; and it is difficult to avoid
feeling that much of what we will characterize as his
arrogance is connected with want of clarity at this point.

The statements we have been discussing are religious:
Mill himself says so. The principle of utility enjoins
maximization of the finest things of which men are
capable: and this is what Mill means by the Religion of
Humanity.

Not only does all strengthening of social ties, and all healthy
growth of society, give to each individual a stronger personal
interest in practically consulting the welfare of others: it also
leads him to identify his *feelings* more and more with their good.
. . . He comes, as though instinctively, to be conscious of himself
as a being who *of course* pays regard to others. The good of

others becomes to him a thing naturally and necessarily to be attended to, like any of the physical conditions of our existence. . . . This mode of conceiving ourselves and human life, as civilisation goes on, is felt to be more and more natural. Every step in political improvement renders it more so, by removing the sources of opposition of interest, and levelling those inequalities of legal privilege between individuals or classes, owing to which there are large portions of mankind whose happiness it is still practicable to disregard. In an improving state of the human mind, the influences are constantly on the increase, which tend to generate in each individual a feeling of unity with all the rest; which, if perfect, would make him never think of, or desire, any beneficial condition for himself, in the benefits of which they are not included. If we now suppose this feeling of unity to be taught as a religion, and the whole force of education, of institutions, and of opinion, directed, as it once was in the case of religion, to make every person grow up from infancy surrounded on all sides both by the profession and the practice of it, I think that no-one who can realise this conception, will feel any misgiving about the sufficiency of the ultimate sanction for the Happiness morality.[1]

Utilitarianism is capable of attracting all the sanctions given to any other religion. The clerisy performs the functions once performed by the clergy: one of the ideal objects to which attention should be turned, in substitution for the ideal object of Christianity, is altruistic elevation of the feelings. To describe by the word 'morality' the injunction to identify oneself, not just with one's own interests, but with the whole human race is, says Mill, to claim 'too little for it; [it is] a real religion, of which as of other religions, outward good works (the utmost meaning usually suggested by the word morality) are only a part, and are indeed rather the fruits of religion than the religion itself'.[2] The theological temper and theological interests of Mill can-

---

[1] *Utilitarianism*, p. 195.
[2] *Three Essays on Religion*, p. 109.

not be doubted. What sort of temper was it, and what was the content of the position?

Mill did not have, in any normal sense, a religious upbringing. In his father's house there was no religion. So far as Mill came in time to take religion seriously, there was disagreement, but his hostility to prevailing orthodoxies involved no breach with the religion of his family. It involved, on the contrary, self-confident protest against what he thought of as the mediocrity of prevailing opinion. Unlike Sidgwick, Hobhouse, Leslie Stephen, and other post-Christian agnostics of the generations following, Mill had never, properly speaking, had a religion. Through his wife's family and connections he had indirect knowledge of various sorts of English dissent: through Romantic literature he understood something of the sentimental religion of the heart. But of the religion of the churches he was ignorant, and profoundly contemptuous. That is not to say that his contempt was always expressed. There is about Mill's treatment of Christianity a caution more suitable to tactical proselytizing than to earnest propagation of the truth. His attempt to distinguish the teachings of Christ (for whom he expressed admiration) from later theological accretions (for which he did not) was probably a genuine expression of his own conviction. The recurrent assertion that Utilitarianism does not conflict with the Christian message may well have been part of a deep-rooted desire to reconcile all truths with all others. There seems no reason to doubt the sincerity of the assertion that 'other ethics than any which can be evolved from exclusively Christian sources', so far from totally superseding Christian teaching, 'must exist side by side with Christian ethics to produce the moral regeneration of mankind'.[1] These positions are genuine intellectual conclusions

---

[1] *On Liberty*, p. 45.

which follow consistently from the need for comprehensiveness and 'antagonistic modes of thought'; it may be no more than muddle which neglects the significance of the Christian claim to know the truth about God's nature, and supposes that 'the good' from Christianity can be retained once this central claim has been rejected. Yet, it is difficult to avoid feeling that the strength of contemporary Christian feeling, and the damage Mill feared from attacking it openly, increased the ambiguity of his public statements. The specifically religious writings do, indeed, go a long way to expose his attitude towards Christian claims. They were, when they were published after his death, less hostile to Christianity than Mill's friends had expected, but they were more hostile than anything he published in his lifetime. What emerges from them is commitment to general cultivation, and recognition that *some* Christians have *some* part to play in providing it. There is no unambiguous statement of his willingness (in certain circumstances) to see Christianity rejected altogether, and nothing to match the assertion, made privately to John Sterling in 1831, that 'in France, where Christianity has lost its hold on men's minds . . . a Christian would be positively less fit than a St. Simonian (for example) to form part of a national church'.[1] Mill was conscious of the power of Christian feeling in England: reluctance to play a part in destroying, without replacing, an established doctrine, was one consideration which made him unwilling openly to reject Christianity. It is, however, possible, at least, that genuine reluctance was strengthened by tactical awareness that moralists who wanted to propagate *his* general injunctions would do well to take pains to 'adopt (as far as without hypocrisy

[1] J. S. Mill to John Sterling, Oct. 20–22 1831. Elliot, *Letters of J. S. Mill*, vol. I, p. 5.

they can) those means of addressing the feelings and the conscience to which a connection with Christianity has given potency'.[1]

However, if we are to consider what Mill thought (in private) as well as what he published, one may say that, for Christian theology, and for the developments imposed by generations of theologians on the moral message of the 'founder of Christianity', Mill had a fundamentalist's aversion. Mill is not, in these circumstances, it might seem, promising material for theological comment. Nevertheless, for Mill, no less than for any other Victorian moralist, religion was a major preoccupation. He was hostile to Christendom, not indifferent: his agnosticism (if that is the right word) has about it a quality of inquisitorial certainty; he displays at considerable length an active theological concern with three of the most important questions with which theology has to deal—the character of Nature, the knowability of God, the existence of evil: if we wish to understand the character of his utilitarianism, it is necessary to understand what he has to say about them.

It is essential to understand that, in Mill's view, Nature—the world untouched by Man—is not in itself good, and does not testify to the existence of a Good God. It may be held to testify to the existence of an author of Nature, the Creator of the world, 'a Being of great but limited powers . . . of great, and perhaps unlimited intelligence':[2] but contemplation of Nature as it is without human intervention lends no weight whatever to the belief that the Creator of the world is a being of great moral power. 'There is no evidence in Nature', he writes 'for divine justice, whatever standards of justice our ethical opinions may lead us to recognise. There is no shadow of justice in the general arrangements of

[1] *Three Essays on Religion*, p. 194.   [2] *Ibid.*

Nature: and what imperfect realisation it obtains in any human society . . . is the work of man himself . . . making to himself a second nature far better and more unselfish than he was created with'.[1]

Nor does the dogmatic religion of the churches help to establish that God's character has moral quality. The doctrine of atonement and belief in Hell (which Mill thinks inessential additions to the original body of Christ's teaching) make it difficult to accept the Christian God as a tolerable moral being. Not content with creating a world in which there is no moral order, God subjects men to injustices and indignities, punishments and torments which they have not merited. Christ, regarded by Mill as the founder of Christianity rather than the Son of God, was, indeed, a being of great moral grandeur: but how is it possible to reconcile His 'beauty and benignity and moral greatness' with 'recognition . . . [in Christianity] of the object of highest worship in a being who could make a Hell, and who could create countless generations of human beings with the certain foreknowledge that he was creating them for this fate'? 'Is there' he asks 'any moral enormity which might not be justified by imitation of such a Deity? And is it possible to adore such a one without a frightful distortion of the standard of right and wrong'?[2]

Reconciliation of these two standards—the standard of the highest human aspiration (as seen, among other places, in Christ's teaching) and the nature of the Creator of the World—has central relevance to utilitarianism *and* religion. Mill's epistemology is empirical and anti-transcendental: we have seen sharp philosophical comments directed at the practical effects of Intuitionism: this hostility extends to its theology. Mill's religion is a religion of Sense-Experience. It insists, against

---

[1] *Three Essays on Religion*, pp. 113–14.   [2] *Ibid.*

transcendentalist claims to direct knowledge of God's nature or direct intuition of his goodness, that men can know God's nature only as they know other natures—i.e. phenomenally. Men can, says Mill, know the effects of other men's wills, not other men themselves, and can do no more than *infer* their characters from them. In the same way, we can know God only by inference from the effects of his works, not by knowledge of his character in isolation from its consequences. Our knowledge of God, therefore, is relative, not absolute, the outcome of a particularly human activity, not the infusion of a Divine afflatus or ignition of a Divine spark. It follows from this that, although we know little about God, what little we do know must be described in the language we apply to men. Words must not be used to mean one thing when applied to God, and another when applied to his creatures. Divine action must be judged by the standards we apply to human actions; we must avoid the temptation to twist words like *good* and *bad* in order to represent the evil inherent in the order of Nature as the beneficence of God's Providence.

Unless I believe God to possess the same moral attributes which I find, in however inferior a degree, in a good man, what ground of assurance have I of God's veracity? All trust in a Revelation presupposes a conviction that God's attributes are the same, in all but degree, with the best human attributes.

If [Mill goes on] instead of the 'glad tidings' that there exists a Being in whom all the excellencies which the highest human mind can conceive, exist in a degree inconceivable to us, I am informed that the world is ruled by a Being whose attributes are infinite, but what they are we cannot learn, nor what are the principles of his government, except that 'the highest human morality which we are capable of conceiving' does not sanction them: convince me of it, and I will bear my fate as I may. But when I am told that I must believe this, and at the same time call this being by the names which express and affirm the highest human morality, I say in plain terms that I will not. Whatever power such a being may have over me, there is one thing which he shall not do: he shall not compel me to worship him. I will call no being good, who is not what I mean when I apply that epithet to my fellow creatures: and if such a being can sentence me to hell for not so calling him, to hell I will go.[1]

It may be legitimate to argue that men cannot grasp the character of God's Providence or the nature of His Goodness, to maintain, that is to say, a total agnosticism about it: but Mill is emphatic about the need, in practical moral judgement, where God's work is under consideration, to reject what is unknowable as being, for that reason, irrelevant. That which is knowable—the phenomenal world—is alone relevant: moral standards there must be the outcome of human judgement because they are created by human wills through human words. Knowledge of goodness, and judgement of what is good, are part of the human effort to improve, elevate, ameliorate the Nature which God has provided as the area of human activity: and we must *always* use 'good' to mean what we mean by it in normal usage.

The proposition, that we cannot conceive the moral attributes of God in such a manner as to be able to affirm of any doctrine or assertion that it is inconsistent with them, has no foundation in the laws of the human mind: while, if admitted, it would not prove that we should ascribe to God attributes bearing the same name as human qualities, but not to be understood in the same sense; it would prove that we ought not to ascribe any moral attributes to God at all, inasmuch as no moral attributes known or conceivable by us are true of him, and we are condemned to absolute ignorance of him as a moral being.[2]

Whatever goodness God himself may have, however greatly human goodness has been increased in earlier

[1] J. S. Mill, *An Examination of Sir William Hamilton's Philosophy* (1865), London 1878, pp. 128–9.
[2] *Op. cit.*, pp. 134–5.

stages of civilization by men's belief that God supports particular moral systems, it is an anthropocentric and specifically human standard which ought now, in the Religion of Humanity, to determine men's judgement of the right courses to take in the struggle against evil.

Mill's religion, then, is not a supernatural one. Its authority does not depend on supernatural sanctions; Mill is anxious to establish that morality can be damaged when stress is laid on the supernatural character of its authority. He does not deny that supernatural religions have in the past—especially in the theological phase of human history—buttressed the laws and conventions of particular societies. Religion has, to a certain extent he admits, been useful in providing that measure of social solidarity which stable societies need. Supernatural religion, however, is not *essential* to maintaining a stable morality. Morality (Mill means *any* morality) can maintain itself so long as parents, public opinion and the educational system are committed to maintaining it. Though religion is usually credited with 'all the influence in human affairs which belongs to any generally accepted system of rules for the guidance and government of human life',[1] it is not the religious content which is effective, but the fact that *something* is taught, and taught definitively. 'Vast efficacy belongs naturally to *any* doctrine received with tolerable unanimity as true and impressed on the mind from the earliest childhood as duty', and 'a little reflection will . . . lead us to the conclusion that it is this which is the great moral power in human affairs, and that religion only seems so powerful because this mighty power has been under its command'.[2]

Not only, moreover, is religion unnecessary, it is often in these respects positively damaging. A healthy society

[1] *Three Essays on Religion*, p. 78.   [2] *Ibid.*

85

is not, in Mill's picture, a society where men accept a morality because it has been accepted in the past, or because it has been promulgated by unreasoning authority. The only homogeneous society worth considering, in Mill's writing, is a society where *all* men are actively engaged in recurrent reasoning about the character of goodness and its relevance to the problems by which they are confronted. They may defer to the authority of cultivated minds, but rational men will do so only because the cultivated mind does better than most men what all men would do for themselves if they could. Deference to this sort of authority is not arbitrary: it is a natural exercise of the practical reason, and will disappear once the minds to whom deference is given cease to give evidence of superior cultivation. Deference of this sort is rooted in human judgement and reason, but does not supersede them. Deference to supernatural authority induces an arbitrary, unreflective conservatism, and a damaging tendency to silence rational argument. Human reasoning will be maintained only by constant effort: the effort will not be sustained if deference predominates. The moral consensus must be neither arbitrary nor imposed; it must be the outcome of self-conscious reflection. Reflection should be guided by an education in Humanity: this process of inculcating moral attitudes and positive knowledge will speed the spread of the three most important pillars of untranscendental religion—utility, disinterestedness and mental cultivation. These are the comprehensive ethical injunctions, but they are at no point free from human scrutiny: they are, so far from being the conclusions of supernatural religion, the basis of the most wholly terrestrial of all—the Religion of Humanity.

The Religion of Humanity has, for its chief end, the principle of utility in the widest sense. It is a religion, in

Mill's view, because it performs the social functions of religion, and commands authority because it contains, in a peculiarly powerful form, 'the essence of religion, the strong and ardent direction of the emotions and desires towards an ideal object'. 'The ideal object' is a benevolent desire for the elevation of humanity. To establish that the Religion of Humanity is *a* religion does not, however, establish that anyone is *obliged* to conform to its precepts. Obligation will seem weak unless it is not only *a religion*, but also the only religion worth attending to. If it is not the best religion, then it may be an open question whether its precepts should be obeyed: and apologists who claimed only that it was a *possible* religion would not be thought to have said very much in its favour.

It is sometimes supposed, by Mill's critics and by his friends, that Mill was not a proselytizer—that, since his objective was as wide a variety of human accomplishment and disposition as possible, he could not have believed in a best religion. Mill's liberalism, it has been supposed, is an invitation to *every* sort of human experiment. Examination of Mill's words, however, makes this seem unlikely. He wished, at one level, to encourage scrutiny and questioning of every established habit, religion and institution: he was opposed to every sort of received (arbitrarily received) orthodoxy. Nevertheless, his liberalism does not involve replacing authoritative commitment with a vacuum. He is claiming to free men from wrong, inadequate or arbitrary postures: he is not freeing them from religious postures altogether. On the contrary, he is committed, not merely to believing that the Religion of Humanity is *a* religion: he is committed also to believing that it is 'a better religion than any of those which are ordinarily called by that title'[1]; and,

---

[1] *Three Essays on Religion*, p. 110.

since this is a large claim of the greatest consequence, we must ask why he supposes that he is entitled to make it.

He feels entitled to make it, in the first place, because the Religion of Humanity is the outcome, not of authoritative dictate, but of the efforts of all those highest minds which, in the course of history, have turned their attention to the problems of human conduct. Mill's view of history shows in some places the impress of an intelligent relativism, but in others he is not only not relativistic, but is positively dogmatic in imputing a monoply of merit in any particular situation to the cause, or person, whose opinions or actions he admires. *On Liberty*, though not the only point at which he establishes a synthetic history for himself, provides the best examples. There he assumes that the history of the world provides evidence of a strand of recurrent resistance to mediocrity, a gallery of enlightened heroes, whose cumulative wisdom and authority constitute a validation of his doctrine. That the majority *can* in some situations be right: that Socrates *was* a corrupter of youth, and that it is by no means clear that *he* is to be respected and his critics condemned, are not, at this point in his argument, positions Mill thinks it desirable to stress. There is, it is true, reiteration of the belief that no man has a monopoly of truth, and that majorities, or dominant opinions, are not infallible; but, if dominant opinions are *not* infallible, nor are defeated opinions either; and it is not easy to see why the opinions of Socrates should necessarily be thought better, when detached from the context in which they were enunciated and the consequences they produced, than the opinions of those by whom he was driven to death.

Whatever we may think of it, Mill believes he can discern an antinomian, libertarian tradition of this kind. He believes that its reflections have provided mankind with an 'ideal object of reverence', and that its general beneficence and rational altruism supply substitutes to replace the sanctions which fear of punishment supplied to the moral dictates of supernatural religions. The fellowship of the best minds, and the moral approbation of humanity, provide, indeed, a secular version of the Communion of Saints: for 'the thought that our dead parents or friends would have approved our conduct is a scarcely less powerful motive than the knowledge that our living ones do approve it; and the idea that Socrates, or Howard, or Washington, or Antoninus, or Christ would have sympathised with us . . . has operated on the very best minds as a strong incentive to act up to their highest feelings and convictions'.[1] It is this combination of certainty that these are the best men, that they are advocating both the *best* and the *same* courses, and that these 'highest minds, even now, live in thought with the great dead, far more than with the living, and next to the dead, with those ideal human beings yet to come', which gives Mill such confidence in them. Not only is the tradition a communion of the best minds, it is also a comprehensive junction of the best doctrines. Mankind, in its constant struggle to improve the world, has, through this work of resistance to mediocrity, enunciated elevated doctrines: the history of mankind is a record of their progressive accumulation. Once gained, truths of this sort are not lost. Once uttered by a powerful moral teacher, they become the permanent possession of mankind: and the process of trial and acceptance, to which all doctrines are subjected, guarantees that, in the highest minds, all that is best in all the best doctrines will be comprehended.

The Religion of Humanity, then, consists of the best doctrines that have been propagated by the best minds,

---

[1] *Op. cit.*, p. 109.

and may, almost by definition, be taken to be, not only a good religion, but the best one. Even if this is so, however, it is still doubtful whether mere assertion that it *is*, would give it binding authority—particularly when the supernatural sanction is rejected. In order to do this, it is necessary, on utilitarian grounds if on no other, to make claims about the consequences of adopting it. This Mill does not fail to do: indeed, so far from failing, he claims for the Religion of Humanity the sort of comprehensive consequence which supporters of almost all religions have almost always made for commitment to them.

We have talked already about *disinterestedness* in Mill's utilitarianism: but it is necessary to repeat once more that the principle of utility and the Religion of Humanity alike induce a higher disinterestedness than any that has ever been advocated by the highest ethical doctrines in the past. *Disinterested* concern for the welfare of mankind is the first, and central, injunction in Mill's practical doctrine, and provides essential direction of the higher faculties towards an 'ideal object'. Disinterestedness has been made part of the higher human ethic: disinterested concern for all humanity provides spiritual and moral satisfaction on the one hand, and fulfilment of human nature on the other. Kant would have agreed: 'in the golden rule of Jesus of Nazareth we read the complete spirit of the ethics of utility'[1]; where the highest minds concur, there can be no doubt of the categorical character of the injunction. As humanity is improved, and desire for immortality diminishes, the Religion of Humanity will be even more appropriate than in the past. 'Mankind can', says Mill, 'perfectly well do without the belief in a Heaven': 'what is odious in death is not death itself, but the act of dying and its

---

[1] *Utilitarianism*, p. 179.

lugubrious accompaniments'.[1] A time may come when 'human nature' will reach the point at which it begins to find 'comfort, and not sadness, in the thought that it is not chained through eternity to a conscious existence which it cannot be assured that it will always wish to preserve'. And when that time comes, so long as 'the Religion of Humanity [is] as sedulously cultivated as the supernatural religions are, . . . all who had received the customary amount of moral cultivation would up to the hour of death live ideally in the life of those who were to follow them'.[2]

The Religion of Humanity has, furthermore, the beneficial consequence of providing greater opportunity than there would have been otherwise, for general participation in human activity and the working of society. Mill does not write, as Marx or Hegel did, about alienation: he is not concerned with the problem in the same form. Nevertheless, he is interested in *participation*, in the attempt to find means whereby those who have recently emerged from feudal or aristocratic tutelage, should feel that they belong in a rationally ordered society. Mill fears the consequence of failing to extend this sense of participation. Nothing can prevent manual labourers exercising an influence over social policy: nothing would be more dangerous than a class of fundamentally uneducated persons making their irrational mark on social habit and governmental action. Mill wishes to cultivate the faculties of the uneducated—because cultivation maximizes happiness, and makes labour more 'salutary' by making the labourer more intelligent: and because education will give, as well as to all other classes of philistines, to this dangerous one also, a sense of participation, not merely in the animal side of life, but in

[1] *Three Essays on Religion*, p. 120.
[2] *Op. cit.*, p. 119.

that higher cultivation of the sensibilities which is essential to rational living. It has been difficult, in a disordered society, to provide the emancipated classes with stable opinions; much industrial labour, in Mill's view no less than in Marx's, is mere drudgery. But if the injunctions of the Religion of Humanity are propagated extensively, greater solidarity will be achieved.

This sense of participation is not just a passive acceptance of authority, the docile assenting to its propositions. It involves active critical self-examination; energetic pursuit in every particular of the closest approximation to Truth. Mill's society is a society of seekers after Truth: Truth has a sacred position in his scripture. He reserves for it the unctuousness which an unctuous religion will reserve for God: he means by it as many, and elusive, things as others might mean by *Salvation* or *the end of human history*. Truth is what all men are seeking, or supposed to seek: it appears in many forms. An essential prerequisite is to see the arbitrariness of habitual commitment for what it is. Self-conscious, rational reflection and the struggle to be free of prejudice and habit (so far as habit had not been renovated by reflection) lead, also, to a communal approach to that form of highest happiness in which knowledge of Truth consists. All men, whatever their class, temperament or social standing, are capable of making the approach. This sort of life 'is even now the lot of many': and 'the present wretched educational and social arrangements are the only real hindrance to its being obtainable by almost all'.[1] The religion has, in other words, an oecumenical quality characteristic of all the world's great faiths.

It is, finally, a comprehensive account of the destiny to which all men should be committed, leaves nothing

[1] *Utilitarianism*, p. 175.

uncertain (at the level with which it is concerned) about the manner of ascertaining men's duties, and is the best of all religions, because it is founded, not on unquestionable supernatural *authority*, but in the needs, desires and higher natures of men. It is utility *and* goodness *and* moral grandeur, the search after truth and the elevation of the sentiments: it is a view of the past and an account of men's duties in it: and an attempt to overcome the limitations of existence by providing rationally binding chains which, slowly but certainly, free men from the arbitrary finiteness of their condition. It is, one may say in critical conclusion, either an arbitrary injunction or a contentless one; but, in whichever light it is viewed, it shows Mill to be, not a meek, fumbling liberal, not a man of 'surprising, gentle humanity'[1] or 'hesitant, sceptical spirituality'[2]: not even 'an exceptionally good . . . truly modest man . . . too gentle to express contempt for other men'.[3] It reveals neither 'an infinite patience', 'catholicity of temper',[4] nor 'single-minded devotion to the cause of toleration and reason . . . unique even among the dedicated lives of the nineteenth century'.[5] It exposes, on the contrary, a socially cohesive, morally insinuating, proselytizing *doctrine*. Mill was a proselytizer of genius: the ruthless denigrator of existing positions, the systematic propagator of a new moral posture, a man of sneers and smears and pervading certainty. It is in this respect that he has now to be considered.

[1] Donald G. Macrae, *Ideology and Society*, London 1961, p. 172.
[2] D. M. Mackinnon, *A Study in Ethical Theory*, London 1957, p. 230.
[3] John Plamenatz, *The English Utilitarians*, Oxford 1958, p. 123.
[4] H. J. Laski, Introduction (World's Classics) to Mill's *Autobiography*, London 1924, p. xiv.
[5] Sir Isaiah Berlin, *John Stuart Mill and the Ends of Life*, London 1959, p. 4.

PART II

CRITICISM

" . . . in the summer before I was going up, your cousin Alfred rode over to Boughton especially to give me a piece of advice. And do you know what that advice was? 'Ned' he said, 'there's one thing I must beg of you. *Always* wear a tall hat on Sundays during term. It is by that, more than anything, that a man is judged.' And do you know" continued my father, snuffling deeply, "*I always did?* Some men did, some didn't. I never saw any difference between them or heard it commented on, but *I always wore mine.* It only shows what effect judicious advice can have, properly delivered at the right moment."

EVELYN WAUGH, Brideshead Revisited (1945), Penguin ed., p. 25.

CHAPTER 5

'ON LIBERTY'

It is desirable to begin the critical section of this essay by defending its account of Mill's doctrine against passages in his writing which suggest that the doctrine was more libertarian, and more simply individualistic, than the present writer has been willing to allow. For there can, at first sight, be no mistaking the libertarian character of the great body of Mill's expressions. Chapter V of *On Liberty* is an assault on the 'despotism of custom', conformity and mediocrity, a sustained plea for eccentricity, diversity and individual liberty. *On Liberty*, as a whole, looks like unambiguous criticism of the tendency, in all European societies, to destroy '[the] remarkable diversity of character and culture' prevailing a century before Mill wrote, the expression of doubt about the tendency said to characterize the education given in Mill's day, 'to bring people under common influences and give them access to the general store of facts and sentiments', and a protest against the 'ascendancy of public opinion in the State'.[1] These criticisms lead to the conclusion that 'the combination of all these causes forms so great a mass of influences hostile to Individuality' that it is only by making 'the intelligent part of the public . . . see that it is good there should be differences, even though not for the better' that the disagreeable situation will be avoided in which 'all deviations . . . from one uniform type . . . [are] considered impious, immoral, even monstrous and contrary to

[1] *On Liberty*, pp. 64-5.

nature'.[1] This must seem plain, and writers may be excused who feel no obligation to probe further.

However, the fact that Mill claims for his doctrine the respectability of Freedom need not make us accept his rhetoric at its face value. Mill was addicted to the rhetoric of Freedom as much as to the rhetoric of Truth: but about both it is necessary to ask questions. In particular, we must ask what it is that freedom is supposed to replace, what it is that individuality is supposed to do, and what sort of individuality it is to which men are obliged to move. For, once these questions are answered, Mill's principles seem no more than preferences for one type of polity and character over another. There is nothing self-evident about his preferences: neither Truth nor variety of human accomplishment are preserves of any particular type; there is no need to credit Mill's principles with greater rationality or necessary capacity for maximizing diversity. To establish this is important. For, if it can be established that *individuality* in his writing includes less than all the ends to which men might want to move, then the principle of individuality is designed to detract from human freedom, not to maximize it.

In order to understand the nature of Mill's purpose, it is essential to avoid detailed entanglement in the principles by which relations between government, public opinion and individual action are to be regulated. Instead, we have to ask why Mill wants their respective spheres delimited. We must examine the *objective* to which the principle is directed, rather than the application of the principle itself. Professor Rees has interesting things to say about its practical relevance. The present writer accepts his view that, when Mill defines the 'principle of self-protection' to mean that 'the only part

[1] *Op. cit.*, p. 66.

of the conduct of anyone, for which he is amenable to society, is that which concerns others', he implies 'a division of conduct into actions which either do or do not affect *the interests* of other persons rather than . . . what has generally been supposed to have been the division, namely, into conduct having or not having *effects* on others'.[1] This is an important distinction. It removes the impression that the principle is so general as to give no advice whatever about its application. Mill, it is true, gives a number of applications in the second part of the pamphlet: but it is difficult to establish *any* connection between this general formulation and the detailed applications.

It is, however, far from clear that the drift of Mill's argument is, on Professor Rees' view, more libertarian than it seemed before. The principle, on his interpretation, leaves the impression, indeed, of being more definitively inquisitorial than on the old. (The interest of a man is not, in Mill's usage, his interest in a vulgar selfish sense: a man's interest is his interest as a progressive being—a progressive being with an obligation to be concerned for the well-being of society as a whole, and to maximize the greatest amount of happiness altogether.) Often, as we have seen, there is no conflict between individual self-interest and the interest of society as a whole, but where there is, the individual's duty is to consider, not his own happiness, but the greatest amount of happiness altogether.)

Now the greatest amount of happiness altogether is not maximized if men insist on following their selfish interests at the expense of general happiness: nor will it be maximized if they follow their lower, sensual natures at the expense of the higher. It will not be maximized,

---

[1] J. C. Rees, 'A Re-reading of Mill *On Liberty*', *Political Studies*, vol. VIII, no. 2, 1960, p. 123.

either, if they refuse to be educated, decline to be persuaded to the rational conclusions enjoined by their higher natures or refuse to give that deference to superiority of intellect which Mill assumes rational, educated men will always wish to give. From this it follows that, if the duty of society (or government) is to restrict individuality (when necessary) in order to maximize general utility, then individuality is likely to flourish only so long as it is connected with the higher cultivation of the sentiments. The sort of social or governmental pressure which might, therefore, be admissible on this principle is more searching than superficial attention to the principle suggests. For, if interference with individual liberty *can* be justified on the ground that interference is in the interest of others, and if the interest of others is taken to lie in producing the greatest amount of higher happiness possible, then the injunction is no less vague than before in defining the *amount* of legitimate social (or governmental) pressure, but much more specific in determining the *purpose* to which interference should be put.

Mill distinguishes, it is true, between actions which do injury to the interests of others, and those which do not; and observes that 'the inconveniences which are strictly inseparable from the unfavourable judgement of others, are the only ones to which a person should ever be subjected for that portion of his conduct and character which concerns his own good, but which does not affect the interest of others in their relations with him'.[1] Social action is not appropriate in these cases. In cases where the interests of other people *are* affected, moral disapproval is desirable, not only of the actions themselves but of the dispositions which produce them.[2] But 'the self-regarding faults . . . are not properly

[1] *On Liberty*, p. 69.   [2] *Op. cit.*, p. 70.

100

immoralities . . . They may be proofs of any amount of folly . . . but . . . the term duty to oneself, when it means anything more than prudence, means self-respect or self-development', and, along with other duties to ourselves, '[is] not socially obligatory, unless circumstances render them at the same time duties to others'.[1] This limits the extent to which Mill will tolerate interference with individuality and might seem to make his principle more libertarian than we are suggesting. But it is necessary to ask: why is liberty to be absolute at this point? why, when no assignable damage is done to the interest of others, should a man be left free to do what he likes with himself? And Mill's answer is, not so much because diversity of individual character is desirable *in itself*, but 'because for none of [these duties to oneself] is it *for the good of mankind* that [a man] be held accountable to [his fellow creatures]',[2] and because 'the inconvenience [which society suffers from self-regarding, self-affecting faults] is one which society can afford to bear *for the sake of the greater good of human freedom*'.[3]

'For the sake of the greater good of human freedom', it may be objected, dismisses the view we are taking of Mill's doctrine, and it must, on the face of it, be agreed, that it does. Again, however, it is desirable to ask what *freedom* in Mill is for, and what is the *good of mankind* to which the convenience of bringing social pressure to bear is to be postponed. When the question is asked in this way, the answer will not be disappointing. For the answer is, as it always is in Mill—general social utility, the end and justification of *all* social action.

General utility for Mill means, as we know, maximization, not of *any* happiness, but of the higher happiness, the freedom of men to engage in rational pursuit of disinterestedness and truth. Maximization of the higher

[1] *Ibid.*   [2] *Ibid.*   [3] *Op. cit.*, p. 73.

happiness comes when men are left free (from mediocre social pressure) to reflect on, and choose, the right action rather than the wrong one. The object of right social policy is to find the best means to achieve this end. 'The merely contingent . . . injury which a person causes to society, by conduct which neither violates any specific duty to the public, nor occasions perceptible hurt to any assignable individual except himself' *does* damage society, so far as it diminishes the stock of mental cultivation.[1] The fact that damage *is* done, however, does not mean that society should interfere. Interference would produce consequences no less disagreeable than the consequences that flow from refusing to interfere: once the differing consequences are compared, interference must be rejected. It must be rejected because, in pursuit of 'the good of mankind' and 'for the sake of the greater good' which 'human freedom' brings, non-interference will be more conducive to utility. Where assignable damage *is* done to the interests of others, then the assignable damage outweighs the damage done by restriction of individual liberty, and punishment, or disapprobation, *has* to be imposed. But where assignable damage is not done (or, perhaps, Mill might add, cannot be measured), then men are more likely to maximize utility (despite the inconvenience) by allowing full individual liberty, than by preventing the damage a free man may do by perversely misusing his freedom.

For, even when men are free of governmental or social disapprobation, society still has means of inducing them to act rationally, disinterestedly and with a view to maximizing utility. Because the obvious, formal (and perhaps, in a way, Mill thinks, crude) agencies of public pressure are not used, it is not, therefore, to be supposed that public pressure cannot be brought to bear. Nor

[1] *Op. cit.* p. 73

does Mill think that pressure ought not to be brought to bear. Pressure ought not to be contemporary society's mediocre pressure to conform to ill-conceived, unsystematic prejudice. Nevertheless,

the existing generation is master both of the training and the entire circumstances of the generation to come; it cannot indeed make them perfectly wise and good . . . but it is perfectly well able to make the rising generation, as a whole, as good as, and a little better than, itself. If society lets any considerable number of its members grow up mere children, incapable of being acted on by rational consideration of distant motives, society has itself to blame for the consequences. Armed not only with all the powers of education, but with the ascendancy which the authority of a received opinion always exercises over the minds who are least fitted to judge for themselves . . . let not society pretend that it needs, besides all this, the power to issue commands and enforce obedience in the personal concerns of individuals, in which, on all principles of justice and policy, the decision ought to rest with those who are to abide the consequences.[1]

The best way of achieving a rational consensus, in other words, is to leave men as free as possible to be led into it by rational education. To maximize freedom can, in some circumstances, do damage to utility, but not as much as would be done by restricting it. When the damage done by leaving a man free is clear and assignable, then he must, regrettably, be punished: but where no assignable damage is done, then the *only* rational way to maximize utility is to leave men's minds absolutely open to the working of rational education—because it is only through rational education that unforced assent to the right means of determining the right course of action will take root.

Mill does not, in his *Applications*,[2] emphasize these conclusions, though he believed that education should be

<hr/>

[1] *Op. cit.*, pp. 73–4.   [2] *On Liberty*, ch. 5.

compulsory. But Mill was attempting in *On Liberty* to protect the élite from domination by mediocrity. How he would have applied his principles in a system where the élite had triumphed, and to what extent it could have operated individualistically where a 'rational' consensus had prevailed, is another question. *On Liberty*, in the form in which it was written, so far from being an attempt to free men from the impositions of *all* doctrine, is an attempt to free them from customary, habitual, conventional doctrine. Convention, custom and the mediocrity of opinion are the enemies in Mill's mythology: the freedom he gives is given in order to subject men's prejudices to reasoning authority. *On Liberty* does not offer safeguards for *individuality*; it is designed to propagate the individuality of the elevated by protecting *them* against the mediocrity of opinion as a whole. Convention, custom, habit and public opinion are never to be trusted: all history has been a battle against them. History shows them to be oppressive: oppressions of this kind must be resisted. Once the oppressive consensus has been removed, a better one must replace it: but it would be foolish to expect an imposed consensus to achieve the objects which a rational consensus might. Mill, in fact, had grasp of an important truth—that it is no use *expecting* success from imposing a consensus by force, but that does not make him abandon the attempt to have a consensus. On the contrary: the consensus imposed by mediocrity is bad, and liberty in relation to *it* ought to be as great as possible. The means of achieving a rational consensus will not be discovered by pursuing the intuited views on which conventional opinions depend. But that does not alter the fact that the purpose in allowing men liberty, the justification of individuality, is not diversity in itself, but diversity informed by the rationally agreed education the clerisy alone can provide. Education is desirable and self-development an obligation, because both maximize the same sort of happiness. Mill, in short, feared democracy and loved individuality, not so much because individuality would induce diversity, but because, by breaking up existing rigidities, it would make the world safe for 'rational' education, 'rational' thinking and the assured leadership of the 'rational clerisy'.

CHAPTER 6

THE AUTHORITY OF
THE CLERISY

The direction of Mill's doctrine having been established, it remains to ask what attitude should be taken to it. And the first position to which an attitude should be taken arises from Mill's commitment to claim extensive authority for the clerisy. Consideration of the functions of the clerisy raises important questions about the relationship between political philosophy, political practice and the nature, and men's knowledge, of moral Truth. These questions are important in establishing the character of Mill's teaching, and of first consequence in assessing its value. To accept Mill's view is to capitulate in advance, not so much to his political philosophy, as to his political style. Superior minds are supposed to be free from the confused uncertainties of practice: the clerisy is a body of superior minds; its practical authority is grounded on the fact that this is so. Mill is consistent in wishing, on the one hand, to relieve the agents of doctrinal rectitude from the difficulties inherent in exercising political power, whilst, on the other, ensuring that society gets the benefit of their wisdom. At some times the clerisy is to be more directly political than at others, but at no point are its members to be engaged in what is normally meant by the conduct of politics. They are, it is true, to sit in Parliament, but even in Parliament the intellectual élite, so far from being compelled to calculate possibilities and nurse majorities, is conceived to be a body of educators whose chief function is to emphasize the fact that general reasoning and rational discussion are essential prerequisites of intelligent government.

Political practice, however, involves making decisions, taking chances, arriving at choices between one course of action and another, often in conditions of extreme uncertainty, often where no one course is self-evidently preferably to any other. It involves doing this under pressure, in all societies, from factors which do not relate to the 'intrinsic merits' of the decision under consideration. Calculation of possibility is not the whole of political practice, but, without it, the practice of politics is impossible. Political decisions are decisions to do things in particular times and places; *intrinsic* merits are inseparable from *effective* ones. Moralists who are interested in the *merits* of decisions, but not their feasibility, and who forget that the 'merits' of decisions include not only the policy they are designed to further and the motive they embody, but the use to which they are put, ignore an important dimension. All practical amelioration involves amelioration in specific circumstances: moralists who affect detachment of this sort produce as a consequence recurring tautology or contentless slogans. Rousseau's injunction to obey the General Will is a tautological assertion that it is right to do what it is right to do. Marx's plea to end alienation by ending history is a slogan designed to free men from the unavoidable limitations of their condition. These are obvious examples. But Mill's injunction to defer to the rational authority of the clerisy is no different. It too involves the assumption that rational determination of particular political questions can be made without the limitations inseparable from particular situations, and that rational determination of this sort can be the responsibility (in his case as in Marx's) of those who are supposed to be equipped, by intellectual capacity, philosophical authority and historic destiny alike, to make it. Nor does Mill's rejection of universal precepts relieve him of criticism on these accounts. The objection to *his* position is not the objection Macaulay raised to James Mill's abstract Science of Politics. Mill meets these objections, but his position is objectionable still. The objection raised here stands whether the rule of practice formulated on each occasion by 'instructed minds' is 'framed from the data of the particular case' or not. Whether the rule framed is general or specific, its status is the same, because Mill expects rules to be supplied whose merits are self-evident, whatever the personal, political difficulties in the way of putting them into practice. 'Instructed minds' argue to the *merits* of cases: because an improved Sociology will enable them to do so more effectively in the future, a new phase of politics, and a new 'Art of Life', can, in Mill's view, be expected.

Political cases, however, cannot, in this detached sense be argued on their merits. Resolution of particular problems involves consideration of the circumstances as they are and calculation of the consequences as they will be: and *all* political decisions are particular ones. They involve, sometimes, charm, bluff, cunning, brazenness and luck, and these do not figure in Mill's Art of Life. Without them, politics has not begun; without them, practical rules are merely slogans. Slogans induce sensations of certainty, which in most circumstances has its uses. Certainty of this sort, however, has limitations, of which ignorance of practical limits is sometimes one. Contentless slogans, like recurring tautologies, can justify *any* action 'elevation' is taken to support: injunctions which are intended to overcome the limitations in which all action is involved, may end by suppressing disagreement altogether. It is not *necessary* that they should:

consequences yield no more certainly to dogmatic language than to any other. 'Self-evident, elevated rationality' need not be a prelude to dictatorship, but it can be; and Mill's certainty, no more than Marx's, tells certainly what happens when attempts are made to free politics from the uncertainties in which politics are involved.

No doubt breadth of view, elevation of sentiment and political imagination are, in some circumstances, desirable: but imaginative political conceptions, to be *politically* effective, have to become 'practical problems'. No doubt Mill was right to dislike 'diminutive practical politicians', but it is not clear, when he says so, whether he has distinguished between the limitations inherent in all political action and the limitations of a particular manner he happens to dislike. Imaginative politicians have to achieve office if they are to do what they want to do. They have to do this as much as 'diminutive practical' ones. The ways to office and authority are numerous, and one way is to *seem* a person of large conceptions. Vagueness, mistiness and generality of manner are sometimes aids to success, but they are not necessarily so. Imaginative politicians help to determine the political climate, but each group's or generation's judgement of political possibility is determined by diminutive practitioners also. Once practical agreement is reached about the direction in which society should move, diminutive politics predominate: once diminutive politics begin, 'diminutive practitioners' matter as much as anyone else. They matter as much in a democratic system as in an authoritarian one, and Mill's assumptions are as irrelevant to the conditions he wished to replace as to the conditions he wished to replace them by. There is, in fact, no other way of governing: the difficulties this way involves are not overcome by implying that there is.

To claim that there is is, moreover, in no way to ensure that the claim can be made effective. The clerisy may indoctrinate through education: elevated minds may infuse elevated sentiments. But infusion of principles does not ensure control of consequences. To enunciate one set of principles rather than another is to ensure that *some* impact is made on political practice: but it ensures neither that general agreement will follow, nor that principles produce the consequences that are desired. Elevation of sentiment provides no guarantee of effective government: the superiority of superior minds is not always accepted without questioning. Effectiveness involves exercising power as a man wants to exercise it to the ends to which he wants to put it, and depends on his being in a position to exercise it in the first place. This depends in turn to some extent on chance, to some extent on the intrinsic merits of measures and men, to some extent on the willingness of the political community to defer to the title by which those who want political authority take steps to claim it. To claim authority is not necessarily to achieve it: to succeed in practice (in persuading men to follow) is to say nothing about the intrinsic merits of the course to which they have been persuaded. Nor does effective imposition of a doctrine say anything about its relevance in explanation.

Equally, however, to see that nothing of *explanatory* consequence follows from a practical doctrine is to say nothing about its usefulness in practice. The higher political slogans are almost all expressed in words which are used by political philosophers, but the fact that they are, when considered philosophically, philosophically inadequate, in no way detracts from their practical value. Elevated minds will give elevated advice: elevation implies detachment, and Mill may, if he wants to, ground their political authority on the fact that it does.

To impute merit to superiority of this kind, and claim authority for it, can sometimes be effective. Not always, however. Not all men like elevation of mind. Elevation of mind is, indeed, often distrusted. By itself it launches no ships, makes no friends and commands no power. Ships are launched, friends made and power commanded by qualities commoner than this. Moral immaculateness, no doubt, is respected, but moral immaculateness commands no more respect than wealth, character or social status. Nor, if elevated minds did command power, would they necessarily be free of the difficulties with which all power is invested. So far as Mill failed to see this, his analysis was defective: so far as his *clerical* claims ignore it, the idea of a clerisy was defective; though, since anyone who offers political advice has to cut through some of the uncertainties in which political practice is entangled, one need not criticize Mill, on practical grounds, for doing so.

Nor would advice given by the clerisy necessarily be worse than advice given by the territorial aristocracy whose authority it was designed, to some extent, to supersede. It would not necessarily be better: between the consequences to be expected from one manner of reaching decisions adopted by one set of rulers and the manner adopted by another, there will be no necessary difference. If some rulers find it convenient to adopt Mill's manner and others Palmerston's, many factors besides that one will determine the efficacy of their conduct. Where consequences are in question, the manner is, if not indifferent, then often of secondary importance, and realization of this is one point from which political philosophy takes its start. All these allowances may be made, and, in considering Mill's politics, should be. But, once they have been made, it is necessary to add that, if realization of this *is* a point from which explanation takes its start, then Mill did not get very far in giving explanation. If Mill had affected to offer practical advice only, and sustained it with rhetorical gesturing, his writing might have been as influential as it was. Mill, however, does not confine himself to this. He offers practical guidance, and, in doing so, fulfils what he thinks of as explanatory obligations. He supposes that practical advice is validated by philosophical and sociological explanation, but, in fact, it is not. The injunction to disinterestedness is supposed to be connected with the fact that morality is in some sense a recognition that the interests of others deserve consideration as well as one's own. Whether the stimulus is interested or altruistic, as explanation this view has merit. But no injunction follows. To accept it is to say nothing about the motives by which men should feel obliged to arrange their moral conduct. To grasp the fact that arrangement of relations with other men is an unavoidable facet of social life, is to have grasped nothing of importance about the manner in which these arrangements should be approached. What moral action is, and what our motives should be, are different questions: authority in the first carries no authority in the second. Explanation of this kind validates *no* line of political action. Its business is to take political action as the subject for explanatory consideration, to take, even, its own practical consequences—in order to see what correlations exist between the purposes politicians illegitimately deduce from its statements, and the effects these purposes produce in practice. To misuse the propositions of political explanation may, on occasion, be a useful practical activity. Most politicians do this sometimes and some politicians do it more than others. But when one finds it done by a philosopher; when one finds a philosopher allowing it to dominate, and deflect, the structure of his explanation; when, finally, one finds persuasion to moral revolution justified by reference to *philosophical* authority, then one must say that philosophy has been corrupted.

Now Mill's errors about the authority of explanation were, as we saw in Chapter 3, not simple ones; nor were their effects confined to philosophy alone. They were, on the contrary, central to Mill's political doctrine, and to his idea of a university. Intimately connected with his view of the function of explanation was the assumption that the business of a university is to provide an education in general culture. General culture, as conceived by Mill, involves enunciation of moral principles by which action should be guided, and deliberate propagation of moral commitments. Mill did not suppose that universities were the only places where moral indoctrination should be given, but he supposed indoctrination to be a chief function of a university. To this a number of objections may be raised: in the first place, that it makes of a university a dogmatic seminary. For this view of the function of a university, there is something to be said. It is not a view that is often argued in contemporary Britain, but that does not mean that it might not, in some circumstances, be sensible, or that it is not, on many occasions, assumed. Nor is it one to which the present writer would necessarily be opposed: it may well be as easy, within the framework of dogmatic liberalism as within the framework of any other doctrine, to ensure that the explanatory responsibilities of academic faculties are fulfilled. If, on the other hand, it is open to the present writer to reconcile *his* view of the function of a university with Mill's general claims, it is difficult to believe that Mill could. Mill claims at one point that 'it is beyond [the] power [of schools and universities] to educate morally or religiously', that 'moral and religious education consist in training the feelings and the daily habits' and that 'these are, in the main . . . inaccessible to the control of public education',[1] but it is far from clear that his intentions were as limited as this makes them seem. Mill, also, it will be remembered, made it his purpose to 'root out [from university education] . . . not any particular manifestation of [the dogmatic] principle . . . but the principle itself of dogmatic religion, dogmatic morality, dogmatic philosophy'. There is, however, no reason to suppose that Mill's erosion of *existing* dogmas was calculated to free universities from 'the dogmatic principle' altogether. There are liberal dogmas as well as Christian ones, and Mill gives expression to them. 'Relaxation of formularies' may, as he said at St Andrews in 1867, have been 'the tendency of the age',[2] but relaxation of some formularies was a preliminary to imposition of others. One new one was to urge that 'diversity . . . of opinion among men of equal ability . . . who have taken equal pains to arrive at the truth . . . should . . . be a warning to a conscientious teacher that he has no right to impose his opinions authoritatively upon a youthful mind'. Another was that 'an University ought to be a place of free speculation'.[3] A third injunction, to the undergraduates of St Andrews, was 'whatever you do, [to] keep, at all risks, your minds open',[4] and, if 'destined for the clerical profession . . . to use your influence to make [the] doctrines [regarded as essential to remaining in orders] as few as possible[5]'. A fourth was that 'we should not consent to be restricted to a one-sided teaching'—leading to the conclusion that clergymen 'who put a large and liberal

---

[1] *Inaugural Address*, p. 76.   [2] *Op. cit.*, p. 84.
[3] *Op. cit.*, pp. 82–3.   [4] *Op. cit.*, p. 83.
[5] *Op. cit.*, pp. 83–4.

construction [on church articles]' should remain inside the church 'so long as they are able to accept its articles and confessions in *any* [my italic] sense or with any interpretation consistent with common honesty', lest 'the national provision for religious teaching and worship . . . be left utterly to those . . . who, though by no means necessarily bigots, are under the great disadvantage of having the bigots for their allies . . .'[1]

If, in providing general culture, enunciation of this sort of principle is the function of a university, then it must be said that *freedom of enquiry*, if it is to prevail, is to prevail in a restricting way. Any set of general principles excludes some other set; any set of intellectual injunctions involves rejection of many others. *Freedom of enquiry* is an intellectual injunction, which inhibits commitment to injunctions hostile to it. To reject 'authoritative' imposition of opinions is to affect to reject 'express' dogmatic 'teaching', but it is doubtful whether it does. 'An university' may, as Mill says, 'exist for the purpose of laying open to each succeeding generation . . . the accumulated treasure of the thoughts of mankind'; a teacher of moral philosophy may be obliged not to 'take a side, and fight stoutly for some one against the rest', and it may be that 'it is not [his] business to impose his own judgement, but to inform and discipline that of his pupil'.[2] These assertions seem reasonable, but are hardly compatible with others. A teacher, in Mill's view, has, for example, an obligation not just 'to inform and discipline his pupil', but also to 'direct [the various ethical systems he offers for consideration] towards the establishment and preservation of the rules of conduct most advantageous for mankind'.[3] 'The moral or religious influence which an university can exercise consists' he adds 'less in any express teaching, than in the

[1] *Op. cit.*, pp. 84–5.   [2] *Op. cit.*, pp. 77–9.   [3] *Op. cit.*, p. 78.

pervading tone of the place'. Nevertheless, it consists, he thinks, in both, and commitment to offer both involves rejection of alternative commitments. 'Whatever [a university] teaches', he says, 'it should teach as penetrated by a sense of duty . . . making each of us practically useful to his fellow-creatures . . . elevating the character of the species itself; exalting and dignifying our nature', and we may agree that a university which is permeated by this combination of humanistic self-righteousness and rationalistic antinomianism would be likely to produce a type of undergraduate different from the type produced by a university which is not. That, however, does not make it essential that it should. It may be that 'there is nothing which spreads more contagiously from teacher to pupil than elevation of sentiment',[1] but elevation of sentiment guarantees neither knowledge of truth, accuracy of expression nor professional competence: and it is difficult to see why Mill takes it that this kind of elevated sentiment should, in these circumstances in a university setting, be thought so obviously desirable.

Nor does the authority of Mill's humanistic erosion of ecclesiastical religion gain greater authority by being thought of as General Culture. General Culture has to be maintained generally. If accepted throughout society as a whole, its principles have to be accepted on the authority of whoever proposes them; there is no need to attribute to universities special authority in doing so. Universities always have had, and always will have, some impact on the religion, morals and conduct of the societies of which they are a part: if that were all Mill meant by General Culture, universities should certainly help maintain it. General Culture, however, for Mill, does not mean learning to be cultivated in the accomplish-

[1] *Op. cit.*, pp. 76-7.

ments of the society in which an undergraduate is growing up (with a view to improving cultivation in the future). General Culture means, on the contrary, critical reflection and mental doubt, sceptical scrutiny of existing habits, and, where habits are judged to be irrational or wrong, deciding which habits should replace them. It means *following the argument whithersoever it leads us*; it means subjecting all conduct to critical scrutiny, and it means rejecting assumptions which halt argument before argument gets wherever it should take us. It means, in short, moral indoctrination—and moral indoctrination of a kind which would lead to acceptance of liberal utilitarianism.

Indoctrination, it is necessary to say, is not the business of a university. Universities leave their mark on undergraduates, but they have no obligation to leave a rationalistic one. And not only have they no obligation to do this: to claim that they have the obligation is to misunderstand the obligations they do have. When Mill says that 'the proper business of an university . . . is . . . to give us information and training', he means 'information and training', not just with a view to academic and professional competence, but 'information and training' with a view to forming men's beliefs about the right way to infuse the right content into their moral principles. About this, however, it is impossible to agree. Moral principles are concerned with moral consequences: the distinguishing obligation of a university faculty is to offer explanation, and explanation is best offered without regard for the consequences in which moral guidance is involved. Explanatory competence is not related to moral merit; there is no reason why it should be. Some scholars are good moral guides, others are not; professional competence does not guarantee that any will be. Universities seldom have moral standards higher

117

than the societies of which they are a part: moral standards do not depend on universities as much as Mill supposes. All citizens have moral obligations towards their neighbours: dons share them in relation to their pupils, and some dons have greater responsibility than others. Academic faculties have no obligation to society at large (except to offer the best academic work possible); universities have no obligation except to provide the best education they can manage, and it is only because Mill thought them useful counter-weights against existing churches (because, indeed, he wanted to make them substitute churches) that he thought they should have.

Now Mill's idea of a university was not accidental. It arose from the view he took of the status of the clerisy, and the nature of its practical authority. The clerisy had, in relation to moral and political conduct, as we saw, in his view, two functions to perform; its authority rests on the combination of the two. Instructed minds provide, on the one hand, sociological explanation and prognostication, and, in doing so, free 'diminutive practical politicians' from the limitations of their method. They provide, on the other hand, the general principles with which philosophy is concerned, and by which practical conduct should be tested. Sociology, by itself, says nothing about the ends to which action should be directed, the *philosophia prima* of practice by itself says nothing else: but the two bodies of teaching together are able, on any particular occasion in Mill's view, to provide authoritative guidance. Since this combination of functions cannot have authority more necessary than each has separately, we shall, first of all, consider them separately.

Sociology, we found in Chapter 3, meant, in Mill's mind, some sort of historical explanation. His description of the nature of historical explanation was defective, but it became clear that, whether defective or not, his view involved the assumption that most sociology was, in some sense, history. If this were all Mill claimed for sociology, this half of this chapter would not be necessary. Philosophers would long since have corrected Mill's account of the character of historical explanation, if they had not ignored it altogether. *Philosophy of History* would have been thought a solecism, but a solecism of this kind would not have aroused suspicion. Mill, however, claims more than this—with deliberate political intention. He claims for Sociology, in the first place, predictive value, which in itself raises doubts. Mill was aware of the criticisms to which his position could be subjected, and took pains to cover the more obvious ones. His caution about the possibility on any particular occasion of actually making a prediction which will turn out to be accurate was designed to meet the criticisms of those who believed that prediction is possible in principle, but almost always difficult in practice. His recognition of the tangled character of *all* political situations, the diversity of causes which affect the development of particular societies and the complexity of treatment to which scientific statements have to be subjected before providing guidance or prediction, all show him guarding himself against the view that simple, one-to-one prediction is impossible where complicated societies are concerned. Nevertheless, when all these merits have been discovered, one finds, in Mill's account of the nature of Sociology, severe limitations—a misunderstanding of its relevance, a failure to grasp the limited character of the explanation its subject-matter is capable of yielding.

The question we are asking is: what range of relevance has Sociology? and the answer depends on the prior answer to the question: what does Sociology explain? Sociological laws, in Mill, depend on the results of historical investigation. Historians normally suppose that what they are explaining is *the past*, but one expects a philosopher to ask what, in this context, *the past* means. Is *the past* a thing historical explanation uncovers? or is *the past* something historians *assume?* Do the documents and buildings in the present reveal *the past*: or do they provide opportunity for an exercise which, whether it does so or not, historians call *reconstructing the past?* Assuming that *the past* once *was*, what certain knowledge (if any?) does historical explanation supply about it? and must philosophers accept historians' assumptions that they do in fact describe *the past?* These are questions of high philosophical interest, and of first significance in establishing a normative, or predictive, Sociology. For if the philosopher does not accept the claim that historical explanation reveals *the past*, then he cannot accept the claim that *the past* offered by historical explanation has relevance to predicting the future.

And the philosopher cannot accept the claim. Historians may feel obliged, when they write books, to write as though they explain *the past*. The stimulus to accurate investigation is the idea of knowing how things were at a particular time and place. *The past* is taken to mean (and not only by historians) *whatever historians describe:* so long as the quality of historical writing is maintained, there can be no objection to historians sustaining themselves with slogans of this sort. Nor, in practice, is it objectionable to find historians offering accounts, not just of limited particular pasts, but of *the whole past moving into the present.* Historical writing is of two kinds— explanation of a limited piece of what is taken to be *the past*, and writing which describes the outline of what is taken to be *the past leading into the present.* Specific writing about a specific piece of *the past* presents no problem, and professional historians tend to be happiest when dealing with it. Outline sketches of one particular past leading into another, but not into the present, are conventions with which historical writers are well-acquainted. They present no difficulty, and imply no ability to predict. Outline sketches of the past which lead into the present do, however, in some hands imply ability to predict, and since Mill seems to mean by *Philosophy of History* an undertaking of this kind, it is desirable to say a few words about it.

For Mill, Philosophy of History is the superior kind of historical explanation which, by establishing general correlations between historical variables, enables men to analyse the constitution of the present and, therefore, to predict and control the future. Mill assumes that the subject-matter for explanation by Philosophy of History is *the past leading into the present*, and that Philosophy of History is the range of higher explanation which is reached when the *facts of history* have been subjected to comparative generalization in the light of sociological reflection. It is, also, the act of discerning trends, discovering where things are going and predicting where they will go in future. It is real knowledge, because, Mill assumes, historical writing does show *the past moving into the present*, and because, in making his crude distinction between the facts of history and their interpretation, Mill assumes that *the facts of the past* are agreed, established realities with a positive existence of their own about which historians have positive knowledge.

This, however, fortunately or unfortunately, is not the case: nor is it a useful way of describing historical explanation. *The whole past which leads into the whole present* is so vast that no one historian can offer explanation comprehensive enough to command unanimity of assent from others. The emphasis given by each historian to each element in the historical process varies: the amount any historian knows about the whole is small. If he knows about a subject as large as the history of the British Economy, the subject-matter on which knowledge is based is likely to be limited, and his account of those parts of his study which have not been intensive, blurred. This was so in Mill's day (when the body of historical knowlege was small): it is so today. The *facts* of *the past* do not, in historical explanation, have an agreed, positive existence of their own. The phrase *historical fact* may mean one thing or another: we will discuss in a moment what it does mean. But whatever it means, historical fact cannot in historical writing be divorced, at any significant level, from the interpretation by which it it surrounded. Not only do *the facts themselves* explain nothing, but *the facts* cannot, at any level but the most elementary, be divorced from the view that is taken of them. Definitive history is an impossibility, and mere accumulation of fact, if it is possible at all, should not be mistaken for it. The facts an historian considers will, to some extent, determine what he thinks important, but what he thinks important will determine what he considers. Interpretation is not something imposed on the facts, but the form in which the facts come to the historian who interprets them.

Nor are *the facts* of which interpretation is given either *the past itself* or *the past moving into the present*. The subject-matter for historical explanation cannot, for philosophical purposes, be said to be *the past*. It is, on the contrary, the documents, buildings, letters and memories of living persons in the present, on which historians perform their operations. Historians take the subject-matter and explain that: they do not have *the past* and explain it. They assume the past, even, in a sense, create it: but they have no contact with *what actually happened*. From this it follows that, if their knowledge is knowledge, not of the past but of the documents, then comparisons between pieces of historical explanation and predictions based upon them, are comparisons and predictions, not about *the past* or about *the present which has emerged from it*, but about the accounts which historians have given of the documents. And it follows from this that the only authority attributable to historical explanation is in explaining the subject-matter, and its only predictive value in anticipating what would be found if the same, or other, historians go to the same subject-matter again.

By generalizing from ideas found useful in fabricating one piece of historical explanation, it is often possible to stimulate historians to apply the same sort of explanation to a subject-matter on which it has never before been tried. Generalization is a methodological tool, useful in stimulating historians to widen their range of explanation. Explanatory tools which have been found useful in understanding subject-matters from *the past* may be helpful in understanding the world in which an historian is living. His picture of the world suggested by the sixteenth-century documents may, in its broad generality, be helpful in inferring from whatever he knows of the twentieth-century world, *the twentieth-century world as it is*. Sensible historians will not suggest that the pictures should be the same: nor will the emphasis in each be identical with the emphasis in the other. But, so far as it indicates the scope and possibilities of human action, generalization of this sort is helpful in marking, as it were, the limits within which the generalizer takes it that historical explanation will have to do its work. 'It could not possibly have been, or be, like that' is as serious a criticism of a particular piece of historical explanation as comment which comes from scrutiny of the documents themselves.

There are, however, two further points to be made In the first place, predictive prognostication (which Mill admits to be rough) does not follow necessarily from historical or sociological explanation. Historical or sociological explanation is explanation of a subject-matter according to whatever body of explanatory hints seems suitable to the historian who is giving it. The historian, seeing the dead documents, reads them: because he has some idea what range of possibility the documents could suggest, he is able to explain them. The range of possible explanation is not derived from historical or sociological study alone: it *is* the experience of the historian. It is his view of the world, which is more extensive and informal than anything he gets from history or sociology. But if historians do not get their *view of the world* from history alone, are we to conclude that, in formulating such views, they have authority greater than the authority of men who have not engaged in these activities? Are we to infer, indeed, that, in predicting the future of the society in which they live, historians or sociologists have (by virtue of their expertize) any authority at all? Prediction may be undertaken, of course, as an academic exercise, to provide verification of the usefulness of sociological generalizations. If those who offer explanation find this sort of prediction academically useful, there can be no objection to their doing so. No doubt a sociologist who is right on enough occasions about the future will be attended to (by some people at least), but this could be said also of anyone (sociologist, historian or not) who happened to get it right. There is no need to stake out exclusive, professional claims, and if this is what Mill was attempting to do, then Mill was wrong. Even when prediction does turn out to be right, uncertainty is sufficient to be contested. Political prediction on any serious scale is, as

Mill admits, uncertain, but if it *is* uncertain, then it is idle to claim from most men, or political leaders, necessary deference to the authority of minds which are in no position to be unanimous.

The second point to be made is that historical or sociological explanation, when properly given, is always specific. What it does is to take a subject-matter for explanation, and explain it. A subject-matter consists of specific documents and specific buildings: all that can come from considering them is specific history. Specific history is lit with light from many sources: the only *necessary* preliminary is a fertile mind. At some stage in the life of any historian, there has to be a period of general reflection, a stretching of the mind, in which what he takes to be the right range of explanation gets expanded. This process does not have to be systematic. But whether systematic or not, the sources of general reflection, even for historians and sociologists, are not necessarily historical or sociological, and need not arise directly from academic experience at all. They may be called *general* reflection, because they are not concerned with history or sociology (as we are), but they will have *specific* reference to something. Historical or sociological explanation is what happens when a mind which has been fertilized in this way turns to explaining a specific subject-matter in an historical way, and when, by naming names and considering a unique relic, it shows what consideration of the relic suggests.

Now Mill knew perfectly well that the subject-matter for historical explanation was specific, and each piece of the past unique; he knew that, whatever the similarities between one event and another or the development of one society and another, each presents in some sense a unique challenge which has to be answered by specific response. The ridicule to which Macaulay subjected his father's abstract Sociology ensured attention (if nothing else did) to the limitations of mere generality. In spite of this, Mill's view of historical explanation contains two important errors. It supposes, firstly, that generalization has value apart from its relevance to the specific subject-matter to which it might be applied, and general sociology authority superior to the bodies of explanation on which it depends. And it assumes, secondly, that General Sociology is not explanatory merely, but predictive also, and that the *generality* of its statements in some way guarantees predictability. Since these are errors crucial to the claim that sociology can supersede the 'empirical politics' of 'diminutive politicians', it is necessary to examine them closely.

The claim Mill makes for Philosophy of History is illegitimate. By *Philosophy of History* the present writer means philosophical explanation *by philosophers* of what historians do when they write history, but we shall not, for the moment, criticize Mill for failing to use the phrase in this way. Assuming (with him) that Philosophy of History is something *historians* do, then, we may say, he supposes Philosophy of History to be general distillation of truths about correlations between the various factors which have operated in the history of mankind. This, however, raises difficulties. Even if we use the phrase in the way Mill used it, *Philosophy of History* cannot mean what Mill took it to mean. Even if it *is* something historians do, it cannot be that. Philosophy of History is taken by Mill to be something more than a methodological aid to historical writing: but if it *is* something historians do, it cannot yield more than historical activity can yield. Historians, as historians, can make historical statements, and historical statements involve specific explanation. *General distillation of truths about correlations between the various factors which have operated in the history of mankind*, if it is an historical activity at all, is not made more valuable by being more general. Its generality depends, indeed, on specific explanation as a source, and should aim at specific explanation as its object. Philosophy of History, in fact, even on Mill's terms, has none of the general authority Mill claims for it. The fact that its statements are general does not make them historically more valuable: the practice of calling them *Philosophy* does not make them more *necessary*. Historians do not *need* a Philosophy of History. Systematic correlation of historical variables is useful so far as it facilitates explanation of the subject-matter, but it has no other utility besides. The historical obligation has been fulfilled once the subject-matter has been explained: the sources of explanation relevant to any particular occasion are numerous. General Sociology and Philosophy of History can be two of them, but it is not necessary that they should be. Some historians find *systematic* organization of hints inhibiting. *Systematic* promulgation is optional, something historians may be stimulated by if they want to. Systematic promulgation gives generalization no greater authority than the applicability of the generalization permits: all judgement of usefulness is determined by relevance to the subject-matter for explanation. Philosophy of History has no greater authority than any other means of fabricating explanatory concepts, and needs, as much as any more informal method, to be validated by specific application. Without a specific subject-matter, Philosophy of History, in Mill's sense, has no authority; if anything, it is a phase of methodological stretching preliminary to specific explanation of whatever needs to be explained. And if this is the extent of *its* authority, it must be the extent of the authority of General Sociology. General Sociology depends, in Mill's view, on the Philosophy of History; but, if it does, it too must be seen as a body of hints which have informal use, but no authority, until they have been put to work on the particular subject-matter which calls for explanation.

Mill, in fact, supposed that he increased the authority of historical explanation by calling it Philosophy of History or General Sociology, but there is no reason to think he did. Historical explanation is historical explanation, whatever it is called: historical generalizations are aids to explaining historical subject-matters, however desirable that they should be something else. Sociology, in Mill's usage, is historical explanation, or it is nothing, but history is not made more impressive by being called Sociology. And even if Mill had limited the scope of General Sociology as closely as he should have done, he would still have exaggerated its usefulness. Articulated sociological laws are not necessary to historical explanation. Historical explanation is explanation given by historians, and it does not matter how they come to give it. Historians who find comfort in a sociological manner may find sociological articulation useful, but it is not necessary that they should.

Nor does the fact that it is based on Philosophy of History give Sociology authority to offer normative political advice. Philosophy of History is an aid to explaining the subject-matter, not injunction to action or prediction about the future. It is reasonable, in hypothetical sciences, to ask what *would* occur *if* one factor or another were the only ones operating in conditions which have been isolated for consideration. Mill bases Economics on this foundation: to this there need be no objection. Economics, however, is a hypothetical science, whose practical authority is limited by the complexity of the situations in which economic decisions have to be made. Neither Philosophy of History, the *philo-*

sophia prima of practice nor the 'Art of Life' (which is an amalgam of the two) can effect the transition from explanation to injunction: the generality of Sociology in no way makes it easier. The transition, indeed, *cannot* be made: since it cannot, these explanatory activities lack authority in practice. Sociology is not a higher compound of history and philosophy, embracing and superseding both: it is either history *or* philosophy, and in neither case has authority more extensive than theirs.

If General Sociology is not necessary to historical explanation, nor is there any reason to think it necessary to political practice. Just as historians and sociologists do not *need* preliminary, articulated advice about the method suitable to giving historical explanation, so politicians do not *need* professional, sociological advice about the means suitable to conducting *their* activity. They may find it helpful, if they are accustomed to getting their practical bearings by juggling sociological slogans. If a politician happens to have spent his early years as a sociologist, he *may* reach decisions by discussing problems with others whose language and range of interests are the same as his, but that is a matter of temperament and convenience, not a matter of obligation. Nor is this altered by Mill's belief that General Sociology, combined with the *philosophia prima* of practice, will exert political authority when instructed minds promulgate its judgement as self-evident determinations of the higher reason. There is, in fact, no reason to think it will: to think it might is to expect a unanimity which is unlikely to be reached. Between one account of the means suitable to achieve a given end and another, it will not be deference to explanatory self-evidence, or explanatory unanimity, which decides what course a statesman follows, but a combination of *his* confidence in the judgement of the person, or group, which is giving the explanation, and *his* judgement of the desirability of appearing to favour that group in those circumstances at that time. Deference will be given, not to explanatory authority alone (which he may well be incapable of judging), but to the suitability in *that* situation of the act of taking advice from that particular quarter. The decision to take that advice, or attend to advice from that quarter, will be the significant political act, not just the act of enunciating the advice: the reasons which move statesmen to act in one way rather than another will not, in these circumstances, be determined by reference to academic authority merely. Most explanatory sciences suffer the limitation (at times in Mill's eyes, a virtue) of containing within themselves mutually conflicting bodies of explanation. Sociology suffers the limitation (if limitation it is) of containing 'antagonistic modes of thought'. But if there *is* conflict within the professional field, then the authority to which statesmen are expected to defer will not, as Mill thinks, be the authority of the science, but the authority of whatever scientists statesmen happen to prefer. This, indeed, is the difficulty about the claims Mill makes for the political authority of the social sciences—that he does not show how authority is acquired in practice. He fails, in explanation, to give weight to the fact that political deference often cannot be given to agreed explanations—because sociological explanations are seldom agreed, and because elevated minds do not always understand the difficulties which confront those from whom deference is expected. His explanation of the nature of political activity assumes greater deference to elevated sentiments than is common—with the consequence that the claims made on behalf of the 'instructed' sociologist bear so little relation to past, or probable, reality, as to be little more than tactical devices in favour of *his* sort of person. One cannot object to Mill claiming for the altruistic middle-class intellectual a place, as it were, in the sun. One may admire the disingenuousness of the undertaking, the effectiveness of the denigration. Dogmatic certainty of this kind has it uses. But if we are to measure Mill's certainty by philosophical standards: if we are to ask how far philosophical argument supports Mill's reasons for preferring his doctrines to any other, our admiration must be tempered. For his claims to authority rest not, as he thinks, on reason, self-evidence and rational reflection, but on arbitrary assertions of authoritative commitments which, if easily embraced by some philosophies, consort oddly with Mill's.

Of the two functions which the clerisy had to undertake, provision of a general Sociology was, in Mill's mind, in origin wholly explanatory. It became persuasive as Mill wrote, but did not initially suffer the objections to which bare claims to normative authority would lay it open. However, if Sociology became persuasive, as it were, inadvertently, the *philosophia prima* of practice involved from the start deliberate designation of political purposes. The *philosophia prima* of practice is the activity through which the intellectual élite chooses general social principles; and Mill's position is philosophically inadequate at the point at which he justifies the truths on which these principles are founded. It is inadequate, because he is in two minds about the character of the ends to which he is trying to persuade. He seems, at some times, to suppose that they have the characteristics of a religion, and at these moments comes nearest to recognizing their power, and limitations. At others, he supposes that they are, in some sense, self-evident, or will obviously be thought so by those who give them unprejudiced 'rational' consideration: at these points, so far as he supposes them not to be a religion, he lacks a certain transparency. If they are, as he says, a religion, then they must have the characteristics of a religion. It may, in Mill's sense, be irrational to believe that God is a good God and Christ his Son, but it is no less 'irrational' to believe that the 'highest minds, even now, live in thought with the great dead, far more than with the living, and next to the dead, with those ideal human beings yet to come'. Any belief (and particularly the words in which a belief is expressed) may look absurd to those who do not share it: it is idle to expect to offer *reasons* which will justify it to other people. It is idle to expect the practical consequences of believing to be correlated in any useful way to the intensity, or integrity, of the belief. A man believes whatever he can: whatever judgement is taken to be ultimate, the manner of believing is relevant in judging his merit. But the act of believing does not in itself provide guarantees that conduct will be improved, or that others are obliged to believe also. A religion is the expression of a hope, the acting out of a commitment to believe that certain statements are truths about the nature of existence, the character of the universe and the scope of men's obligations in it. They appear to the religious as the necessary, self-evident boundaries of the world in which he lives. Capacity for doubt has a place in this world and fanatical certainty has a place also, but capacity for doubt must stop short somewhere if a religion is to be maintained. No particular necessity and self-evidence, however, is guaranteed to perpetuity. The perennial difficulties can never definitively be concluded. Religious commitment, like any other, is commitment in a particular time and place: opinions vary: whatever commitment is accepted is as arbitrary as variation can make. It is always *possible* to take another point of view: commitment to one does not make it less *possible* to replace it by another. Some theologies embrace as many rejected positions as possible: one theology is sometimes distinguished from another by nothing more radical than the emphasis the constituent elements receive. Emphasis can easily be shifted: the direction of a doctrine can easily be changed. The testing point in any religion is the point at which rejected positions emerge for reconsideration, and nothing philosophy does can mitigate this aspect of the chances to which all religion is subject.

In one sense Mill understood this. At the same time, there is an important, and fundamental, sense in which he did not. Mill gave considerable attention in the *Examination of Sir William Hamilton's Philosophy* to Hamilton's and Mansel's view of the doctrine of the Relativity of Knowledge. Neither Hamilton nor Mansel questioned this doctrine: both, indeed, were enthusiastic supporters. Mansel, in particular, was a Kantian who drew from Kant's writings Christian conclusions which Kant cannot have intended. From Kant's philosophy he concluded that the form of epistemological relativism which had been applied to scientific reasoning, could be applied to moral reasoning also. If reasoning about the natural world is conditioned by 'the forms of thought', he argued, moral reasoning must be equally, and, if it is, absolute knowledge of moral duty is impossible. If the 'forms of thought' infuse human elements into attempts to establish the content of *Moral Duty*, then reason does not have knowledge of *Duty-as-it-is*, and if moral knowledge is not knowledge of reality, Enlightenment could be less 'rational' than its exponents think. If this is so, its criticism of Christianity may be questioned, and its claims to self-evidence rejected. Kant was right to exhibit 'consciousness . . . as a Relation between the human mind and its object', and this conception,

once established [was] fatal [in 'the speculative side of the human reason'] to the very conception of a Philosophy of the Absolute. But by an inconsistency scarcely to be paralleled in the history of philosophy, the author of this comprehensive criticism attempted to . . . exempt the speculations of moral and religious thought from the relative character with which, upon his own principles, all the products of human consciousness were necessarily invested. The Moral Law, and the ideas which it carries with it, are, according to this theory, not merely facts of human consciousness, conceived under the laws of human thought, but absolute, transcendental realities, implied in the conception of all Reasonable Beings as such, and therefore independent of the law of Time, and binding, not on man as man, but on all possible intelligent beings, created or uncreated. . . . As a corollary to this theory it follows that the law of human morality must be regarded as the measure and adequate representative of the moral nature of God;—in fact, that our knowledge of the Divine Being is identical with that of our own moral duties;—for God is made known to us, as existing at all, only in and by the moral reason: we do not look upon actions as binding because they are commanded by God; but we know them to be divine commands because we are bound by them. . . . Amid much that is true and noble in this teaching when confined within its proper limits, its fundamental weakness as an absolute criterion of religious truth is so manifest as hardly to need exposure. The fiction of a moral law binding in a particular form upon all possible intelligences, acquires this seeming universality, only because human intelligence is made the representative of all. I can conceive moral attributes only as I know them in consciousness: I can imagine other minds only by first assuming their likeness to my own. To construct a theory, whether of practical or of speculative reason, which shall be valid for other than human intelligences, it is necessary that the author should himself be emancipated from the conditions of human thought. Till this is done, the so-called Absolute is but the Relative under another name: the universal consciousness is but the human mind striving to transcend itself.[1]

The Relativity of Knowledge, was, then, a prominent part of the Intuitionist philosophy (as Mill recognized): Mill's criticism of Intuitionism is, not that its exponents deny the doctrine, but that, having accepted it, they do not realize its implications. For if, he says, moral knowledge *is* conditioned by the 'forms of thought', then we should take pains to reject the temptation to impute to our relative, limited intuitions of goodness, any necessary, universal relevance, and must avoid claiming for established moral orthodoxies the indefeasibility which intuitionists in practice claim for theirs. This is a reasonable criticism: Whewell, Hamilton and Mansel, whilst not claiming *universal* validity for the social orthodoxy to which they were committed, certainly assumed an indefeasibility which they supposed was connected with their philosophical position. So far as they did this, they were inadequate philosophers, though if they had done it deliberately (and not by oversight), their arguments would deserve consideration.

The difficulty, unfortunately, about Mill's criticism, is that, although he was right, as a relativist, to object to philosophers smuggling into philosophy, under the name of conscientious intuition, commitments to styles of conformity which their own philosophy recognized as being 'conditioned by the forms of thought', this is precisely what he did himself. In Chapter 3 we have attempted to show how he came to do it, and to what extent he argued articulately about what he had done. But even if he had argued a good deal more articulately than he did (and distinguished, a good deal more consistently than he wished to, the explanatory function of *science*

[1] H. L. Mansel, *The Limits of Religious Thought Examined*, London 1859, pp. 201–3.

from the normative function of *art*), it is clear that he expected philosophy to provide advice which, if not universal, is, in conjunction with the statements of science, 'indefeasible', and that he makes on behalf of the sociological intelligentsia claims to politico-intellectual leadership which are supposed to follow from it.

It is possible to see the political relevance of this claim. Mill's situation, as a highly articulate, intellectually ambitious member of a middle-class, literary intelligentsia with little opportunity to exercise open, conventional political power, made it likely that *his* claims to political authority would be based, if based on authority they were, on *intellectual* rather than *social* superiority. Looked at from one point of view, that is what his moral and political writings are—claims to supersede leadership based on *social*, by leadership based on *intellectual*, superiority. Nor, for the sake of the present argument, need one adopt any attitude to this claim. If Mill wanted to make it, objection may be raised, but we are not for the moment concerned to raise it. What it is necessary to point out here is that claims of this sort are statements in practice, attempts to exercise power, not part of philosophy: they neither contribute to, nor gain authority from, philosophical explanation. In a normative mode it matters not at all to political sociology, political philosophy, or political science whether Britain is now, or was when Mill wrote, ruled by an aristocracy or a clerisy. There is no *logical* difference between the status of the conflicting claims: explanation can deal equally with either. Philosophy is no better able to help men choose between them because one side claims philosophical authority: there is no reason to think that philosophy would be conducted better if the intelligentsia were politically more effective. Philosophers might have a higher social status: philosophical proficiency might become a road to success: dons might make more money, and universities be better endowed. But these are judgements of political preference, not statements in political philosophy, and there *is* a sense in which to make philosophy an avenue to power may be to corrupt philosophy. In choosing between intellectual superiority and social status as bases for political authority, philosophy, science and explanation should be indifferent: so far as those who offer explanation fail to ensure that it is, they abandon an important explanatory commitment.

And not only has explanation nothing to say about the claims made by a clerisy against an aristocracy, it has nothing to say about the claims of one practical doctrine against another. If the conservative, 'orthodox', socio-religious intuitions of a Dean (Mansel) of St Paul's could not be sustained by philosophical authority, nor could the radical intuitions of Mill. If Christianity does not depend on philosophy for validation or authority, nor does the Religion of Humanity: and if philosophy, legitimately conceived, could not underpin the teachings of nineteenth-century divines, it could not underpin the teachings of nineteenth-century utilitarians either. The indefeasibility of orthodox doctrine rests on whatever authority happens to seem indefeasible at the time, not on philosophical argument: but the indefeasibility, to those who accept it, of rational radicalism, rests on an impression of authority also. To use the word *rational* of a practical posture not only does not guarantee that it *is* rational, it does not guarantee that it has philosophical authority either.

Mill, however, in practice supposes at one level that it does: and we must, for this reason, conclude that the criticism *he* levels against Intuitionism may properly be raised against his position also. His emphasis on the

Relativity of Knowledge is designed to destroy Intuitionist confidence in the categorical character of the dictates
of the conscience: so far as this is a criticism of its adequacy as philosophical explanation, it has merit.
Opinions do vary: habits do change: there *is* no *philosophical* need to suppose that the intuitions of any particular conscience are necessary, eternal or universally
true. But, if they are not this, and if Intuitionism gives
an inadequate account of the nature of binding commitments, Intuitionism may contain an important *practical* truth. It may be giving expression to the view that,
if anyone *is* to be committed to a religion, then he has,
by definition, to think it a true one, and has got to see it
(or a substantial part of it) as the natural, necessary body
of assumptions within which he lives his life. He may,
of course, change his assumptions, and may from time
to time wrestle with the difficulties connected with them.
Doubt is a religious condition: its temptations (at least
as much as the temptations of its opposite) have left their
mark on religious experience. But, whatever the significance of doubt, there is a point beyond which it cannot
be allowed to go if a religion is to be believed, and nothing
Mill says provides binding reasons why anyone should
stop short at his particular dogmas instead of at any
others.

The truth, therefore, which intuitionism suggests, is
that the extent to which a man believes a religion can be
measured by the extent to which he accepts, without
doubt, those intimations of his conscience which suggest that a particular religion *is* binding *and* true. So
far as there is doubt (and so far as recurrent self-
examination is judged to be essential, doubt is likely
to be induced), so far will belief in the religion be
ineffective: so far as *reasoning* attempts to question the
assumptions, rather than develop the implications, of the

religion, so far may self-examination erode it. A religion is believed so far as the believer does not question, or can answer questions about, the authority of the commands which emerge from his conscience. Religion, in this sense, is an unproblematical commitment: the commitment is such that men bind themselves, in hope or expectation, in order to explore its implications and pursue its injunctions—with a view to seeing what God (or whatever) has in store for them. Commitment is the significant word, whether men *have committed themselves* or *found themselves committed.* Much of the truth men think they know about moral duty arises from commitments to which earlier generations have committed *them*selves, though some part arises as each generation, after a measure of limited questioning, chooses, or thinks it chooses, to accept them for itself.

If this view of religious commitment is accurate, little need be said about it, except to point that it does not yield to what Mill means by the questioning of *reason.* The questioning of reason means, in Mill's writing, critical self-examination. Religious commitment, however, though it is a rational act, does not *have* to follow critical self-examination. It *can* follow from it, just as politicians *can* find comfort in sociological discussion, but it is not necessary that it should. It is not necessary to give reasons for commitments of this sort; there is no need to expect any of the reasons a man gives for accepting *his* commitments to be binding on anyone who has not decided to make them. To call for justification of a religious commitment is to call for a further more fundamental statement of a commitment more fundamental than the commitment the religion expresses. It is to ask for the justification of the religion: and to ask for it in such a way that whatever judgement is given involves erosion of the religion itself. It was said, towards the end of the last chapter, that Mill was a proselytizer, and this is what was meant—that his injunctions to *rational* argument and *unprejudiced* consideration, and the attempt to impose *his* standards of rational judgement on religious commitment, were expressions of a demand, binding, he implies, on all men, to submit their religions to the test of *reason*. But if religious commitments are to be subjected to the test of *reason*, in Mill's sense, then, on Mill's assumptions, they are to be subjected to the ends enjoined by the Principle of Utility. The relationship between the *philosophia prima* of science and the *philosophia prima* of practice is not simple, but it is clear: 'promotion of [the] happiness . . . of all sentient beings . . . is the ultimate principle of Teleology', and if it is, then Christian 'ends' must be subordinate to it.

Nor did Mill doubt that this is so. It may, tactically, have been necessary to claim Christ's sympathy for the principle of utility. It may, tactically, in a still Christian country, have been desirable to dignify 'elevation of sentiment' by agreeing that the Christian churches have contributed to it in the past. But, at the same time as the principle of utility is said not to conflict with Christian principles, it is clear that it is not subordinate to them: at the same time as it is supposed to embrace the Christian injunctions, it embraces them only to suffocate them in Mill's discriminating hedonism. If reason, argument, freedom from prejudice and so on inculcate, as the ultimate injunction, maximization of utility, then the ultimate injunction is not the doing of God's Will; and if the attempt to justify Christian commitment will lead Christians to give reasons (instead of prejudices) for their commitments, and see similarities (rather than differences) between the religions of the world, then Christianity must be justified by reference to something more fundamental than the injunction to believe in Christ. This is what Mill expects reason to produce: this 'something more fundamental' is the *philosophia prima* of practice, the activity in which men give reasons for their commitments. If this is so, then Mill is asserting that the *philosophia prima* of practice, the giving of reasons to justify or condemn the ends men choose, not only has authority to justify or condemn religious commitment, but is essential if they are to feel it right to have any commitment at all. Philosophy, in other words, is supposed to be more fundamental than the religion of the ostensibly religious; the arbitrary, prejudiced commitments of religions which decline to justify themselves by reference to general utility are assumed to fall short of the point at which authority can be claimed for them.

Nor is this conflict to be overcome by suggesting that *Christian* rational reflection will reach conclusions the same as those reached by *utilitarian* rational reflection. If that were so, there would be no point in replacing *Christian* language by *utilitarian*. The *content* of Mill's utilitarian injunctions is as nebulous and comprehensive (at one level) as the general injunction to do God's Will: if there really were identity between the two sorts of rational reflection, the desire to maximize right conduct, however conceived, might as easily be met by supporting Christianity as by attempting to supersede it. Mill recognized the utility of Christianity (so far as it increased happiness through social cohesion), but, if it is supposed that the doctrines really are identical in any foreseeable circumstances which Time is likely to bring forth, the assumption is mistaken. Whatever happens in the long run, in any run but the longest, one religion is distinguished from another by a combination of language, manner, ritual, doctrine and moral teaching. A religion which finds no place for prayer and worship, treats Christ as an elevated

man, and contrasts the goodness of man with the
a-morality of God may well be a religion, but the fact
that some aspects of the morality it teaches are compatible with some aspects of Christian morality, in no
way mitigates its opposition to Christianity.

To assert that Christian commitment is arbitrary
would, of course in these circumstances, be a legitimate
practical device: there can be no *philosophical* objection
to using this sort of language in attempting to replace
what a proselytizer thinks an arbitrary commitment by
what he thinks a rational one. If that were all Mill was
trying to do, he would be doing what missionaries always
do do, and could be seen as a missionary of force and
power. It is not, in these circumstances, surprising that
he expects the *philosophia prima* of practice to produce
rational, as opposed to arbitrary, decisions, and supposes that it occurs on a level more fundamental than the
ratiocination of religious commitment. Claims of this
sort are the stock-in-trade of redemptive religions. They
are not to be dismissed by indicating similarities between
the status of so-called philosophical commitments and
the status of religious ones. Religious commitment is not
less religious because it is called philosophy, though it
may, by being called philosophy, in certain quarters in
certain ages, be more effective. The tactical necessities
of the age may suggest the desirability of avoiding too
open an assault on religion as such, but there is no doubt
that Mill, if impelled in the first place by a desire to
replace religion by a social doctrine, came to believe that
the doctrine had all the characteristics of a religion. It
may be that the approbation of the 'great dead' is a
sentimental substitute for prayer, worship and dependence on God: it may be that the Religion of Humanity
at many points wants necessary dimensions. But in
dogmatic certainty and claims to indefeasibility it lacks

none, and in these respects has more than the normal share of missionary power.

Nor does Mill lack what an elevated mind might think of as proselytizing tricks. No tactical device is better calculated to establish the need for some sort of reformation than denigration of existing institutions: if enough mud is thrown often enough, some will stick (whether it ought to, or not). Mill disliked, not all dominant orthodoxies, but orthodoxies which he took to be irrational. His denigration took the form of asserting that dominant opinions tend to oppress, that the passing of the age of fixed opinions was to be regretted and that the rational consensus should be re-established. The criticism was self-contradictory, but that did not prevent it seeming impressive. Not only was the society in which Mill lived criticized beyond the limits of his, or anybody else's, experience, but criticism was sustained by smears which condemn, even whilst affecting to explain. The manner and idiom in which moral criticism is offered is almost always as important as its content. Mill's remarks about character and conduct seem, at first sight and in small measure, moderate and unobjectionable. But uncritical reiteration of phrases like *higher natures, noblest minds, elevation of sentiment, rational, reason* and *Truth,* and the simplicity of the contrast they imply between *their* goodness and the depravity of their opposites—leave the impression of a dogmatically insensitive, self-conscious superiority which, whatever its *claims* to comprehensiveness of sympathy, was incapable of grasping the complexity of the process by which merit must be judged. Mill was one of the most censorious of nineteenth-century moralists. At every turn, denigration of existing society is offered with inquisitorial certainty: the only thing to do to inquisitorial certainty of this sort is to be inquisitorial back. Argument in these circumstances is

143

unnecessary: to argue with Mill, in Mill's terms, is to concede defeat. *Rational* does not *have* to mean *conclusions reached by critical self-examination*. *Prejudice* may reasonably be used to mean *commitments about which argument has been declined*, but to decline argument is not in itself *irrational*. *Bigotry* and *prejudice* are not necessarily the best descriptions of opinions which Comtean determinism has stigmatized as historically outdated: it is not clear what *critical* value should be attached to the tendency to dismiss views Mill happens to dislike because they 'have lagged behind the progress of opinion'. There is not something called *customary* conduct which can be opposed, as simply as Mill opposed it, to conduct that is *rational*. *Customary* conduct can be as *rational* as conduct which is justified with rational slogans. Established morality has conventions of its own: it is possible for these to be *right* or *rational* or *good*. There is no guarantee that they *will* be, but only historical abridgment, or moralizing zeal, can really suppose that between conduct which is offered as the result of *rational self-criticism* and conduct that is *right*, any greater measure of identity can be established either.

Mill supposed that the positions to which he wished to persuade would be validated by rational argument: he would, no doubt, have said that they ought not to provide a basis for social consensus if they could not be. This attitude, however, when not a tactic, is naïve. Doctrines prevail in the social consensus, not just through reasoning, argument and so forth, but from every sort of incidental cause besides: it is difficult to see how this could be otherwise. Fundamental commitments, if they *are* fundamental, have to be accepted in this way: if to accept commitments without argument involves the obligation to explore their implications, there is a point beyond which self-examination is impossible. In the process of acceptance (or rejection), innuendo is as important as 'rational reasoning'—in Mill's writing no less than in any other. Mill knew little in detail about the history of British society in the two hundred and fifty years before he was born. His denigration of its polity and religion was based neither on close observation nor on exact historical knowledge. His experience of the religion, and manners, of the generality of Christians in the society in which he lived was small: his competence to make reasoned assessment of their nature minimal. This did not prevent him speaking clearly, and offensively, about them. Of popular religion and working-class habits (until comparatively late in life) he was ignorant, but not, therefore, silent: about the family lives and personal characteristics of the industrial middle-class and non-political aristocracy, he had no first-hand information. Mill was not the first, or last, sociologist ignorantly to pontificate about the condition of society-as-a-whole, but that does not make his offerings more acceptable. To understand 'a whole society' is an extensive task which the expansion of industrial civilization since 1750 has made it almost impossible to accomplish. There are no short cuts: when short cuts are taken, injustice is almost certainly done. If entertaining history is to be written, injustice may have to be done, but it is less easy to see why political authority should be thought to follow. The assertion that the intellectual consensus had weakened since 1660 involved the assumption that the clergy had maintained it in the Middle Ages (though it is far from clear that it had), whilst the accusations of contemporary 'mediocrity' with which Mill's pages are filled, *could* be justified only by an experience immensely more varied than his was. Mill's historical observations are almost always of this kind. At no point do they descend to detail: at no point does one feel the *complication* of the past as it almost certainly

145

must have occurred. Attention is given to 'dominant strands' in human history—the struggle between *the best men* and their enemies on the one hand, the struggle between *Liberty* and *Authority* on the other—but no questions are asked about the significance of these strands in the whole history of mankind. Even if they were as dominant as Mill imagined, one wonders whether the past was as simple as he made it. Were the opposing forces divided as neatly as Mill suggested? Has there been *one* strand of liberty only? and one of authority? and has the appearance of continuity between the various libertarian movements been of very great consequence in making each effective? Do societies generally become free because the *best minds* have altruistically advocated that they should be? or do they become free because selfish men try selfishly to preserve their interests? Have the consequences of the *best men* and the *noblest doctrines* always been what they should have been? Were Arnold of Brescia, Fra Dolcino, Savonarola, the Albigeois and the Hussites agents of 'the truth' (suppressed by persecution)? and can it really be maintained that 'the Reformation broke out at least twenty times before Luther, and was put down'?[1] Mill made large claims for Comte's historical system, but had the threefold division of the history of mankind historical utility at all? *Was* it 'scarcely too much to say that not one Christian in a thousand guides or tests his individual conduct by reference to . . . the maxims and precepts contained in the New Testament'? Had '[Christian] doctrines . . . *no* hold on ordinary believers'[2]; and was not Mill's history (on which he grounds much consciousness of messianic duty) a flat, dull, unilluminating *Myth* unsuitable even for a mid-nineteenth-century textbook?

This Myth was an 'intellectualist' myth; it assumed

[1] *On Liberty*, p. 25.   [2] *Op. cit.*, p. 36.

that the history of thought is the central chain of human history. The history of thought can certainly matter, but, in order to matter sociologically, it has to embrace, not just the thoughts of elevated minds, but the thinking of society as a whole. Reasoning with a view to action is as important as articulated reasoning with a view to writing. The Church was one source of medieval civilization: courts, castles and agriculture were others. The political authority of the Church was not everywhere effective: the Hildebrandine claims, when looked at in the light of general history, lose some of their importance. Paley was significant of one aspect of eighteenth-century England: Paley's writings reveal little of eighteenth-century England as a whole. Socrates, Antoninus, Washington and Christ (when considered, as Mill wants him considered, as a man) were great men: a lot is heard about them: but so were Napoleon and Alexander, Cromwell and Caesar, and innumerable others about whom we hear nothing. Most moralists assume a past which sustained investigation would destroy: Mill was no exception. But if this may, on practical grounds, be excused, it is desirable to see it for what it was. Mill's history was not superior to the history of his time: it achieved neither high-level reflection nor elevated distillation. All it provided was inadequate explanation of the complexity of human history in the past which, through General Sociology in the first place and the 'Art of Life' thereafter, was expected to validate idiosyncratic injunctions to action in the future.

It is desirable to understand this, but not to be surprised. If a writer believes a doctrine he is promulgating, and feels an obligation to it, he is unlikely to reveal its limitations. Any decision in favour of one doctrine involves negative decisions in relation to others: 'rational' argument alone will not certainly ensure victory for the case that ought to be victorious. Denigration is not, perhaps 'rational'. Denigration is a form of persuasive bullying, but all proselytizers do it, and it would be unreasonable to blame Mill for doing it also. If, however, one need not object to a proselytizer doing this, one should criticize a philosopher when *he* does it, or a proselytizer who claims to be a philosopher in doing it. The Philosophy of Religion arises when reflection occurs on the character of religious belief, the nature of prayer and worship and the characteristics of proselytization, not when the injunctions of one religion are subjected to scrutiny by advocates of a 'better' one. Argument to resolve the question—which commitment should I accept?—has procedures of its own, but philosophy cannot conduct them. One set of binding commitments excludes any other: different men hold different opinions with equal certainty, and *philosophical* resolution of the conflict is impossible. These facts require the heaviest emphasis it is possible to give: a philosopher who grasps their significance will not fail to give it.

Mill, in fact, does give it, but turns it to the wrong conclusion. He assumes that, because it is necessary to pursue these implications in *explanation*, it is necessary in practice to be guided by them also; and the *philosophical* doctrine of the Relativity of Knowledge becomes, in his hands, the basis for practical proposals (in favour of political toleration). It is true that no orthodoxy can know itself to have a monopoly of Truth, but this is a truth which has no necessary consequence in practice. If no practical orthodoxy has a monopoly of Truth, the assertion that Truth ought not to be imposed is a practical assertion which has no monopoly of Truth either. From the explanatory assertion that no practical orthodoxy is certainly true, more practical conclusions than one may follow: it is not necessarily the case that men ought not, therefore, to impose on others their own ideas of what they have decided to accept as true. Moral and political injunctions gain no authority from philosophical explanation and need not be affected by it. The truth (if truth it is) that 'the same causes which make [a man] a Churchman in London would have made him a Buddhist or a Confucian in Pekin'[1] may be useful in historical writing, and is, philosophically, of great importance, but it does not, by itself, impose an obligation to draw any particular conclusion in practice. If all men are in fact men first, and English or Chinese second, they will not necessarily realize it, or be pleased to be told that it is so. If it *is* so, they will not necessarily be able to do anything about it: if they try to act with Pekin in mind as well as London, this will not necessarily make their action more effective in the one, or more relevant to the other. The fact that men are men first, and English or Chinese second, may induce altruistic concern for the well-being of the whole world, but that does not guarantee that the whole world will benefit. The fact that expectations of this kind are likely to be disappointed is not, of course, a reason for refusing to entertain them. It is, however, a reason for thinking that one other practical conclusion, at least, could be drawn—that, if 'the same causes which make a man a Churchman in London would [in fact] have made him a Buddhist or a Confucian in Pekin', he may feel an obligation to protect his identity as a London Churchman, in ways which London Churchmen alone are in a position to understand, so as to emphasize the fact that it is English Christianity he wishes to see developed, not the Religion of Brotherly Love.

The fact is that there is no *necessary* connection between the explanatory statement that moral knowledge

[1] *On Liberty*, p. 16.

is 'conditioned by the forms of thought' and the conduct men ought to pursue in searching for moral truth. A coherent epistemology can accept the reasonableness of the philosophical doctrine, without imputing any consequent obligation, in their own particular fields, to practitioners of subjects other than epistemology. Something may be said for the assertion that 'he who knows only his own side of a case . . . knows little of that', but it does not necessarily follow that 'the rational position for him would be suspension of judgement'. In some finely-adjusted minds suspension is necessary; it is sometimes thought an academic virtue. We need not, however, in matters of temperament, be unduly exclusive. Academic explanation can be given (just as political judgement can be made) from *any* temperament, and by men who take *any* view in the field of epistemology —so long as they surround the subject-matter on which they are engaged with whatever explanation seems relevant to it. Neither ignorance of epistemological doctrine, nor knowledge of it, will necessarily make a man a better historian, physicist, philologist or crystallographer. A man may, in epistemology, be a relativist, and may, in epistemology, see all the philosophical implications of the position. But if he wishes to be an historian, it will not necessarily be desirable to concern himself with them; if he does, it may sometimes be best to dispose of what looks like epistemological hesitation (but is in fact consciousness of the conclusions of earlier historians) through systematic historiographical investigation. Historical explanation requires unambiguous statement of what the historian takes to be *his* truth about the subject-matter which lies before him, and it requires nothing else.

Similarly in political practice. Mill wished to 'supersede empiricism'. If this meant only that Mill thought empiricism a poor explanation of what political practice involves, no criticism would be offered here. Unfortunately, Mill does not confine himself in this way. When he complains about the damage done to political studies by political practitioners, he means not only that explanation must improve its account of the nature of the political process, he means also that men generally (and politicians in particular), should change their method of reaching political decisions. The authority of the *Art of Life* rests on conjunction between the *philosophia prima* of practice and the *philosophia prima* of science (Sociology); to accept *its* principles is the best way of ensuring success in practice, and it is the business of philosophy to define them.

Now definition of this sort of principle is precisely what philosophy is incapable of supplying: the only sort of activity which can, is what is generally called *general philosophy*. General philosophy, today, is frequently said to be dead: its death is frequently regretted, but it is far from clear that there is any reason why it should be. A plea for general philosophy is, in the present context, a plea for moral guidance, and that can be given in other ways with smaller damage to philosophy. It *is* easier, if philosophical writing *is* general, to induce moral elevation, whilst creating the impression of intellectual energy, but it is not unknown for moral advice to creep into professional philosophy also. Nevertheless, assumption of *general* responsibility is unlikely to improve the quality of the philosophical undertaking: the less extensive the philosopher's sense of social obligation, the less likely is he to succumb to the temptation to be something other than he should be. Mill felt a pressing sense of social obligation, which was not confined to his socio-political writings. For Mill, logic was not an explanatory activity merely. Logic, for Mill, was a normative one.

It explained how men ought to conduct discourse, and what criteria should be relevant in it. Mill claimed to know how political decisions should be reached, not just that they are (whatever politicians might think they are doing) reached in the way he describes. He is not just saying that a politician who happens to be a philosopher will find 'empiricism' an inadequate explanation of what he does as a politician: he is saying that the empiricial manner of exercising power is a bad way to exercise power. He is saying that there is a way of acting—empirical acting—and a way of deciding—intuitional deciding—which has bad political consequences: and that *A System of Logic* can rescue the political Art from the limitations those ways of acting have imposed upon it. *Empiricism* and *Intuitionism* are bad philosophies, as much because of their consequences in practice as because of their inadequacy as explanation; but because general sociology and general philosophy, conducted according to the methods suggested in *A System of Logic*, can overcome these limitations, *A System of Logic* must be taken seriously.

This is unacceptable. It is unacceptable because, whilst affecting at one level to keep explanation separate from practice, it in fact confuses the two. Philosophy is part of practice in one sense only—in the sense that it has conventions of its own, limits of its own and functions of its own. Its function is the writing of books, delivery of lectures, conducting of conversations in which discussion is carried on about the nature of the world and men's knowledge of their place within it. It has consequences outside this area, because everything that happens has consequences: but the function of philosophy, and the purpose it serves, is confined within these limits. Philosophical empiricism is a way of describing our knowledge of the world; in relation to politics, it gives a particular account of what men do when they make a decision. Its validity is in explaining the fact that decisions are constantly being made, but it is not a contribution to making them. Nor is its usefulness to be determined by those who make decisions. It is a contribution to philosophy, not to political practice. Sociological, historical or philosophical explanation are pastimes in which statesmen sometimes play a part. But, when they do so, they bring with them no particular authority. The fact that a statesmen thinks empiricism an adequate account of the nature of political action says nothing about his conduct as a politician. It is possible for a statesman, on holiday, to talk empiricist (or, indeed, any other philosophical) language, and yet to act in such a way that philosophical empiricism (or any other philosophical doctrine to which he happened to be committed), would fail to explain the nature of his action.

Nor, if knowledge of truth *is* relative, and if claims to know Truth cannot certainly be known to be true, do men *have* to avoid the temptation dogmatically to assert that this or that *is going to be taken to be the truth.* Overshadowing Mill's pages is the idea that the search for Truth is never to be completed. Overshadowing them is the idea that, if Truth cannot certainly be reached, it must always be approached through intellectual conflict. Mill distinguishes two ways of approaching moral and political Truth—the approach through argument and the approach through force, though it is difficult to see that they can, in any particular society, easily be separated. All social authority rests on an amalgam of force and opinion: this is the case in 'free' societies as well as in authoritarian ones. Force is, in any case, not perpetual, and is never unlimited either. Also, if knowledge of truth is 'conditioned by the forms of thought', it is difficult to see how any one can know that opinions propagated by force are not as 'right' as opinions propagated through critical self-examination. A doctrine which is imposed in the first place by force may, with the passage of the generations, come to be accepted without strain: indeed, in some circumstances there is no other way of getting an opinion (even a rational one) accepted. Nor are conflicts between 'antagonistic modes of thought' *necessary* on the road to Truth. Sometimes they help: to some temperaments they are essential; others they merely distract. Disagreement may remain even after rational deliberation, but men have still to act as though it does not. Occasions arise on which someone has to say that *this* or *that* is going to be taken to be the right social end—and *this* or *that* the right means to approaching it. When governments do this, they do not say 'this or that *is going to be taken to be* the right end'; they say 'this is true', 'that is the law' or 'that is right'. Tactical certainty is often thought necessary: it is difficult to see on what authority anyone should say that it should not be. Infallibility is (as Mill asserts) often claimed, but it is difficult to see why the Infallibility rhetoric should necessarily be thought more objectionable than *elevation of purpose, rationality of method* or the rhetoric of *Truth*.

These considerations obtain whether a moral system is imposed by argument or by force, and whether it is recommended by 'rational' slogans or by 'irrational' ones. In no case is there any *guarantee* that it is right. Parts of it can, in a sense, be verified: within the framework of their fundamental assumptions, men can see their practical obligations more clearly, or less. In considering action suitable to society-as-a-whole, however, the limitations are considerable. All moral systems grow up over the generations: the view each man in each generation takes of the whole range of Social Good is unlikely to be coherent. He will have inherited most of it, and chosen some of it, but, even where a measure of coherence has been imposed, frayed edges almost always remain. Political *principles* are abridgments of the practice of the society in which they arise: *any* abridgment misrepresents. Even when abridgment does not misrepresent, even where enunciation of principle does no violence to the diversity of moral judgement, the mere fact that particular principles have been judged right provides no guarantee that they are. Rightness involves consequences also, and principle provides no security for them.

Nor can critical examination guarantee that political principles are, in Mill's sense, *rational*. Whatever the point at which a man begins to scrutinize his moral principles, some arbitrariness will be discovered; more, however, will remain concealed, and there can be no guarantee that the arbitrariness is a rational one. All moral judgements are involved in limitation of this sort. Each new judgement assumes an earlier one, which has not been subjected to critical self-examination: at each point in the regress, something has been assumed without asking whether it should have been. In these conditions, provision of rationally authorized principles is not so much illegitimate, as impossible: it is not so much dangerous, as inconceivable, that men should subject their fundamental assumptions to the test of *reason*.

Fundamental assumptions, *because* they are fundamental, *cannot* be scrutinized, and are involved in the most extensive arbitrariness of all. The fact that they vary with the generations need not disturb those who pursue their implications in the generation in which they live; the fact that their rightness cannot be established does not make it wrong in practice to act as though it had been. Men do whatever they think it right to do: the fact that opinions vary need not make them any less determined to ensure that particular ones prevail. For all these reasons, therefore, it is impossible to agree that Mill's persuasion to moral and political toleration follows from his philosophical assumptions. It may be impossible to *know* that a moral or political position is right, but that does not mean that rightness is more likely to be achieved if decisions are reached after earnest, comprehensive, high-minded self-examination. Critical self-examination is never *necessary*. Reasons do not *have* to be given for reasons to exist, though reasons exist, whether they are given or not. To demand that they should be, if not just a temperamental quirk, is an arbitrary preference. Each preference seems to those who hold it to be as good as (or better than) any other, but each can be confronted with positions whose authority to others seems in no way less impressive. Preferences will not be maintained if the consequences are bad, but argument (with others) and reasoning (in conflict with other minds) does not more certainly produce *right* decisions, or the *right* outcome, than the habit of riding hunches as far as they will go. Intellectual commitments are obscure in origin, and unpredictable in operation. They come fitfully and unexpectedly: there is no guarantee that they are true. If useful, they fit the circumstances of the time, and the experience of the minds that use them. The success of an explanatory doctrine (or a moral one) depends far less than Mill implies on intrinsic merit (narrowly conceived), much more on the accident of its generation and the circumstances of the moment. The accidents of generation and the circumstances of the moment include whatever men happen at the time to feel obliged to do; men *can* do right *with* force and *without* critical self-examination. There is no guarantee that action of this sort *will* maximize Truth, but there is no guarantee that it will not, and one may be grateful for the fact that this is so.

Nor, finally, is man's fitful grappling with Truth connected in any necessary way with the type of polity Mill wished to see established. The impact made by established political systems on those who enunciate moral and political Truths is devious and unpredictable. Spinoza might not have made *his* contribution if he had not been persecuted: Mill might have made a more perceptive one if he had been. There is no evidence that moral culture depends on liberal institutions, none to imagine that intellectual cultivation depends on more equal distribution of wealth. Aesthetic and intellectual achievement depend on persistent development of the requisite sensibilities, on traditions of professional competence and on patrons or audiences who are willing to be interested, not on the pervading commitment to make men scrutinize their consciences. Any state of society can make *some* approach to cultivation of this sort: cultivation will not be made more possible in the future by claiming for a demanding moral system merits it is unlikely that it could have.

Liberalism, then, for Mill is a means of persuading men to organize society in a way different from the way in which societies have been organized hitherto. It is as aggressive in relation to other ways of organizing society as any other doctrine, and as erosive of existing institutions. It is as erosive, also, of existing moral habits. It assumes that conscientious decisions will usually be decisions contrary to existing practice, and that conscientious decision can be made only by self-conscious reference to 'rational' principle. If one cannot object when Mill, or his followers, claims that liberalism is not like other doctrines, if one cannot, in practice, erode *their* claims by replying that it is, one can point out that dogmatic commitment to doctrines of this sort is neither an explanatory, an academic, nor a philosophical act. The expectations which liberalism raises are as likely to disappoint in practice as those which Marxism has disappointed elsewhere, but to point this out is to provide no reason why liberals should not continue to be liberal. Liberalism in this sense, will continue to rest on the supposition that its truths are self-evident, because elevated reflection supports them, and because superior minds can bridge the gap between practice and philosophy. In fact, however, there is no elevated reflection superior in kind to any other, and there are no elevated persons insulated against the difficulties by which all men are confronted. There are only ordinary persons, sometimes with extraordinary capabilities and sometimes in positions of extraordinary power, who are subject to the conditions to which all men are subject, and whose political, moral and social authority is the outcome of conditions as various as political, moral and social situations themselves.

Nor was Mill ignorant of this. If humanity was to be saved, matters could not be left to chance. For utility to prevail, power must be commanded, and strategy deployed. Mill was reluctant to encourage the use of force. His injunctions are methods of reaching decisions rather than decisions themselves: they are in the first place defensive. Defence, however, is to be the prelude to attack: the clerisy *will* propagate its doctrines. The doctrines may be ways of reaching right decisions rather than right decisions themselves, but the prohibitions are extensive. A society dedicated to 'open-minded pursuit of truth' rejects approaches which are not as 'open-minded'. To welcome one principle is to exclude others. If wives ought to have the status of widows, then they should not have the status of wives. If 'the only part of [a man's] conduct . . . for which he is amenable to society *is* that which concerns others', then 'in the part which concerns himself, his independence *is*, of right, absolute': if there *are* other grounds on which society can reckon one person's opinion as equivalent to more than one', then it would not be the case that 'the only ground on which we [should] do so is . . . mental cultivation'. All avenues at first are to be opened, but only because that is the best way, in the long run, of ensuring that some of them are closed. Free institutions may, in the circumstances in which Mill was writing, have been useful. But Mill did not think them *necessary*. In primitive societies despotism was sometimes desirable.[1] The necessary thing, as Mill perfectly well knew, was not the free institution. The necessary thing was that opinions should be propagated (by rational argument, in his view: by philosophical sleight-of-hand, in ours) in the minds of those who might otherwise maintain opinions as various as the advocates of a free, variegated, self-determining society might be expected to desire.

What, then, do we conclude? In political practice, nothing whatever. We do not imply that the contemporary clerisy should stop fulfilling its journalistic function. Nor do we suggest that connection with the tradition of protest in relation to 'the Dreyfus case, or the Boer War, or Fascism, or Communism. . . . [or] Munich or Suez or Budapest or Apartheid or colonialism or the Wolfenden Report', which Sir Isaiah Berlin claims, to Mill's credit, as evidence of 'three-dimensional, rounded, authentic quality' and 'depth . . . of insight',[2] must

---

[1] *Representative Government*, p. 131.
[2] Sir Isaiah Berlin, *John Stuart Mill and the Ends of Life*, London 1959, p. 31.

necessarily be thought discreditable. Women's suffrage, Franchise reform, criticism of the English in Ireland, defence of Bradlaugh and the enemies of Governor Eyre, hostility to Palmerston and Louis Napoleon (though not, as it happens, to Bismarck) would all, no doubt, have been defended by Mill as salutary challenges to the public opinion of his day. 'Outraging their contemporaries', 'challenging the general complacency', 'in opposition to the public opinion of the day'[1] have for many years now been the virtuous battle-cries of the improving intelligentsia. It has long known that the best way to conceal the arbitrariness of its commitments is to expose the arbitrariness of others. *Hostility to complacency* and *exposure of prejudice* have become orthodox moral postures. *Hostility to complacency* and *exposure of prejudice* are not objectionable in themselves, but the orthodox may find them objectionable yet. For if it is right to encourage the attitude they imply, it is right to expect it to be used against them also. 'Outrage' may be answered with outrage, 'challenge' with challenge, as the question is answered whether *prejudice* or *complacency* better describes that infinite ability to offer as superior, self-evident truths, moral, religious and political commitments whose reasonableness is disputed as much by their own intellectual equals as by a great part of the rest of mankind. If followers of Mill wish to suppose that superior minds can supply rational solutions to political problems without the difficulties from which political problems arise, that is a political illusion which has sometimes been useful. Sometimes, the use to which it has been put has been bad: sometimes it can do damage; when it does, the illusion has to be exposed. Exposure is a political act, not a philosophical one, and the means used may not always, philosophically, be the best ones. What may help

[1] Cf. Raymond Williams, *The Long Revolution*, London 1961, p. 354.

politics may damage philosophy, what may be good for
the clerisy may be bad for scholarship; if those who
bear political responsibility need not put *them*selves out
to meet the requirements of philosophers, philosophers
have an obligation not to put *them*selves out to help
would-be politicians. Philosophical attempts to reconcile the two functions should be rejected: advocacy of
reconciliation denounced. The temptation to build
bridges to bridge gaps which do not need to be bridged
is not one which will easily be rejected, but the difficulty
in doing it does not make it less desirable that it should
be done. Once building has started, bridge-builders are
unwilling to be dismissed: bridges have been built in
the last hundred years which the builders do not want to
see destroyed. Destruction, however, is necessary. Once
destruction has started, argument may begin: once
argument has started, destruction may be seen to have
been right. Destruction is desirable: but argument is
desirable also. Many other instruments *can* be used, and,
no doubt, will be. Many other devices could be employed—with, no doubt, a good deal of success. But, in
destroying even the *desire* to build bridges, 'the first step
. . . is to inspire [bridge-builders] to systematize and
rationalize their own actual creed: and the feeblest
attempt to do this [directed at the least influential
writer] has an intrinsic value: far more, then, one', it is
to be hoped, directed at so influential, dogmatic and
bridge-building a 'philosophy' as the philosophy of John
Stuart Mill.